Stories of Famous Submarines

By the same author

In this series
Famous Arctic Adventures
Famous Lifeboat Rescues
Stories of Famous Disasters at Sea

Novels
Down Donkey Row
The Two Husbands

Travel Books
Rue de Paris
The Gallic Land
Our Guests Paid in Francs
Just Across the Channel
Your Guide to the Loire Valley

Anthology
North African Writing

Stories of Famous Submarines

Len Ortzen

Arthur Barker Limited
5 Winsley Street London W1

ISBN 0 213 16422 1

Printed in Great Britain by
Redwood Press Limited,
Trowbridge, Wiltshire

Contents

Acknowledgements

I am obliged to Granada Publishing Ltd for permission to use an extract from *One of our Submarines* by Edward Young.

Books which have been of much assistance to me will be found in the Bibliography.

I must again express my appreciation and thanks for the help given by the County Librarian, Gloucester, and his staff.

Introduction

The first known instance of an underwater craft being built and used was in 1620, when a Dutchman named Cornelis Drebbel demonstrated his 'little ship' in the Thames and 'calmly dived under the water, while he kept the king and several thousand Londoners in the greatest suspense'. His craft appears to have been a kind of inverted rowing-boat suitably ballasted until just awash; a contemporary stated that it could not dive deeper than twelve or fifteen feet. Drebbel was only interested in travelling submerged, but the next man to experiment with an underwater craft, in 1653, intended it to be used for warlike purposes. He was a Frenchman, De Son, and the hull of his craft was built around a beam tipped with iron – a ram to hole an enemy vessel below the waterline. However, although his craft was completed and put afloat, the machinery to propel it – a paddle-wheel driven by clockwork – proved ineffective.

One hundred and twenty years passed before an attack was actually made on an enemy warship by an underwater craft. This was the *Turtle*, so called because it resembled two turtle-shells clamped together. It was a wooden vessel seven feet deep by five-and-a-half wide, with a hand-cranked propeller, the creation of an American, David Bushnell; it incorporated on a small scale many of the features of a modern submarine.

The *Turtle* had a watertight hatch and was fitted with an internal water-tank which, when flooded, reduced buoyancy to nil. Part of the lead ballast could be released in an emergency; there was enough air to last the one-man crew about half-an-hour, but this could be supplemented through a pipe sticking above water and having a device to close it when the craft was submerged – an early, rudimentary example of the *schnörkel* fitted to U-boats late in the Second World War. A charge of gunpowder was fixed to the outside, enough to send a wooden warship of the time to the bottom. Bushnell's invention was in fact a mobile mine, and had been inspired – like many inventions since then – by a state of war, the American War of Independence.

On a dark night in 1776 the *Turtle* reached one of the British ships blockading New York, the sixty-four gun frigate *Eagle*, without being detected; but the crew, Sergeant Lee, was unable to screw his explosive charge to the hull because of the copper-sheathed bottom. As the *Turtle* was returning on the flood tide, just awash and with Lee standing in the open hatch with his head above water, some British soldiers in a rowing-boat spotted the strange object and gave chase. To increase speed, Lee released the explosive charge and the soldiers abandoned the chase. Another attempt was made later by the *Turtle* but was again unsuccessful.

The first real submarine to be built was the invention of a most versatile and persistent American of Irish descent, Robert Fulton, who was both a painter and an engineer, an unusual combination. He went to Europe and eventually interested Napoleon, then First Consul, in his weapon – a 'plunging-boat' carrying an underwater explosive charge. This, the *Nautilus*, was launched at Rouen in July 1800 and completed her trials at Le Havre a month later. She was over twenty-one feet in length, was shaped like a torpedo, and could carry a crew of three. A small sail rigged to a folding mast drove her when surfaced, and a hand-worked screw-propeller when submerged. Fulton and two men remained submerged in her for an hour in Le Havre harbour, and a few days later covered five hundred yards under water. After trying unsuccessfully to approach some British warships lying off the coast, the *Nautilus* was conveyed to Brest for further trials and with the mission to attack British vessels blockading the port. The *Nautilus* dived in the harbour and reached a depth of twenty-five feet. A sphere filled with compressed air had been fitted which allowed the crew of three to remain submerged for four hours 'without experiencing any inconvenience'. However, the hull made of copper and iron had become corroded and was leaking badly. Fulton wanted to build an improved type, but Napoleon had lost interest and the new Minister of Marine, Admiral Decrès, was against such 'underhand' methods of warfare.

News of the *Nautilus* had reached England and secret agents persuaded Fulton to change sides. Pitt appointed a Commission to examine Fulton's ideas on submersibles and 'torpedoes', but all that emerged from it was an agreement by Fulton that, for a certain payment, he would not divulge his plans to any other power during the next fourteen years. Admiral St Vincent commented that it was 'a mode of warfare which those who commanded the seas did not want and which, if successful, would deprive them of it'.

This was the kind of negative reaction to the development of the submarine which prevailed in official naval circles for nearly one hundred years, until this sinister weapon became a practical proposition at the beginning of the present century.

Before then, in 1850, some very limited success was obtained with a submersible craft. *Der Brandtaucher — The Sea-diver —* was the brain-child of an ex-corporal of the Bavarian Artillery with an aptitude for things mechanical, Wilhelm Bauer. His 'submarine boat' was built at Kiel and was twenty-six feet long, had a maximum beam of eight feet and displaced nearly forty tons. She was built of sheet iron and had sides that were almost straight; a propeller at the stern was geared to a large internal wheel amidships, and there were ballast tanks for submerging. Four glass ports in the sides gave a certain amount of light. By a stroke of genius, Bauer managed to cope with a major difficulty which was never properly solved for the next fifty years – that of maintaining horizontal trim when submerged. Bauer tried to adjust this by means of a heavy weight which could be moved fore and aft along a bar, causing the submarine's nose to point up or down. Her offensive role was to fix mines or explosive charges to enemy ships – at that time, units of the Danish fleet blockading Kiel. But the mere appearance of the *Brandtaucher*, coupled with rumours of her capabilities, was enough to make the Danish vessels raise the blockade and sheer off.

They returned, however, and on a cold February day in 1851 Bauer and two crew put to sea in his ungainly craft. When he judged that he could no longer approach the enemy ships unseen while on the surface, he dived by opening the valves that let sea-water into the ballast tanks. The *Brandtaucher* went deeper than intended, the sides began to buckle under the pressure, the heavy weight broke loose and slid forward. A minute or two later, she struck bottom. Bauer realized that the only hope was to admit yet more water and equalize the pressure inside and outside the hull; the after hatch could then be opened and the imprisoned men escape to the surface in the uprush of air. But when he opened a seacock and began to flood the submarine his two companions thought he had gone crazy. They knocked him down and one sat on him while the other closed the seacock. Bauer argued with them and finally convinced them. Flooding was a slow and nerve-racking process. As the water rose above their waists they shivered and gasped with the foulness of the air. At last the hatch suddenly burst open and the three men shot to the surface, where they were picked up by boats which had located the wreck. They had been trapped below for five hours.

A decade later an underwater craft claimed the first ever victim of this new type of warfare. It was during the American Civil War, and again a blockade by enemy ships gave the impetus to man's inventiveness. The Confederates used a number of cigar-shaped vessels driven by a boiler, with a propeller turned by a man-powered crankshaft, and armed with a ninety-pound charge of gunpowder at the end of a protruding spar, to try and break the Federals' sea-borne stranglehold on their ports. These 'Davids' or 'Hunleys', as they were called after their designer, could submerge only for a short time, during the final stage of an attack. The approach was made very low in the water, with a hatch open to admit air to the boiler and to the men labouring at the crankshaft. This was the cause of several being swamped and sunk, with the loss of more than a score of brave men, including the inventor.

One night in February 1864 a modified 'David' slipped out of Charleston harbour and made towards the blockading squadron. Her commander, Lieutenant George Dixon, was standing with his head out of the forward hatch, just a few inches above the surface. In the cramped interior – sixty feet long but with a beam of only four feet – the crew of eight sat at their cranks. Flickering candles provided some light and would give a warning of diminishing oxygen when the hatch was closed. In the bow was a wheel to work a pair of horizontal rudders or hydroplanes which would force the vessel beneath the surface during the attack. Dixon closed the hatch as he approached the *Housatonic,* a twenty-gun sloop. Her watch were on the alert and sighted a suspicious object in the water. But before the guns could be depressed sufficiently to bear, the object was close and had submerged. The next moment there was a loud explosion, a great hole was torn in the *Housatonic*'s hull, and she quickly sank to the bottom, lying just awash in shallow water. Five of her crew were killed, but so were all nine men in the 'David', which was destroyed by its own 'torpedo'.

So began the destruction and loss of life, the gallantry and self-sacrifice too, which resulted from the development of the submarine. Another half-century passed before this sinister weapon proved itself and initiated new tales of heroism and disaster at sea.

1 The First Kill, September 1914

The internal combustion engine made submarines a practical proposition but in the early years of this century they were still not taken seriously; in fact they were considered highly undesirable by naval diehards of all the major sea-powers. Not only was their offensive ability doubted, but they were regarded as 'pirates' who were infringing the rules of fair play in naval warfare. One British admiral publicly declared that he would hang from the yardarm of his flagship any crew of an enemy submarine who fell into his hands. Even Admiral Fisher, who became First Sea Lord in 1904, regarded submarines chiefly as defensive craft. There had been a number of accidents, and although the number of lives involved was very small, it was generally assumed that the possibility of being drowned was a natural risk of going underwater. During naval manoeuvres there were several 'near misses' between submarines and surface vessels, and the steps taken to reduce this hazard prevented the navy from learning the sort of lessons which war would impose. In 1910 submarines, somewhat like the early motor-car, had to be accompanied by a ship flying a red flag and had to keep their periscope two feet above the water.

In short, the naval high command – British and German alike – had failed to realize the full potential of the submarine as an offensive weapon. When war came in August 1914 it soon proved what a serious menace it could be.

As day was breaking on 6 August 1914 ten U-boats – half of the serviceable German submarine fleet – sailed north from Heligoland with orders to locate the heavy British warships believed to be forming a blockade line between Scotland and Norway. All ten were pre-diesel boats but most of them were equipped with a radio transmitter. One, the *U-9*, was soon in trouble with her petrol engines and was forced to turn back to base. A week later, seven of the U-boats returned to Wilhelmshaven without having sighted any units of the British battle fleet. The remaining two never returned; one had been rammed and sunk by the cruiser *Birmingham*, the other had reported her position on 9 August but that was the last signal she ever made – she had probably struck a mine. It was not an auspicious beginning to U-boat warfare.

The *U-9* put to sea again six weeks later, her mechanical trouble having been corrected and her commander, Kapitänleutnant Otto Weddigen, having taken the opportunity to get married and snatch a short honeymoon. He was a square-headed, hard-eyed, forceful officer with a family tradition of military service, and at thirty-two was one of the most experienced and dedicated German submariners. This time he was setting out on a lone patrol with orders to attack troop transports and their escorts crossing from England to Ostend with reinforcements and supplies for the BEF in Belgium.

The *U-9* was only 188 feet long, carried six torpedoes but mounted no guns, had a maximum surface speed of fourteen knots and a range of 2,400 miles. But when on the surface, the smoke from her tall exhaust stack betrayed her presence, and the long time she took to dive made her very vulnerable in heavily patrolled waters. She could remain submerged for only a few hours and could not safely go down to much more than one hundred feet; while there, she was smelly with noxious fumes and conditions were decidedly unpleasant for her crew of twenty-six officers and ratings. There were only half-a-dozen narrow bunks for the men; others off watch curled up wherever there was space on gear lockers and oily deck plates. But while submerged they were quite safe from the enemy. The depth charge had not yet been invented, nor had Asdic. Mines were usually moored close to the surface to catch the keels of passing ships. The aeroplane was still as much in its infancy as the submarine itself.

Weddigen had no precedents to help him; he had to learn about submarine warfare the hard way. There had been just one encouraging piece of news just before he sailed: a sister U-boat, patrolling off the Firth of Forth, had sunk the light cruiser *Pathfinder* with a single torpedo – the first time one had been fired in anger against a warship.

The *U-9* met a heavy swell as she cleared the Heligoland Bight and headed westward. Her captain carried out a diving exercise and noted the time it took to reach periscope depth – one minute twenty-three seconds. Then he ordered return to the surface, and the *U-9* continued on her mission at twelve knots. But by the end of the day the sea had so built up, with ten-foot waves that broke repeatedly over the *U-9*'s conning-tower, that the small vessel was pitching badly and Weddigen was forced to reduce speed to eight knots. By then he was off the coast of neutral Holland.

An hour or so after dark the first lieutenant, Johannes Speiss, reported the compass out of order; the heavy swell had caused it to 'wander'. Weddigen sent a man on deck to take a sounding. Twice he swung the lead, and each time the line showed seventeen fathoms. In the control room Weddigen and Speiss exchanged looks, then bent over the chart. They should have been in waters ten fathoms deep; instead, the *U-9* was miles off course and farther out into the enemy-patrolled North Sea than was good for her.

The faulty compass did not worry Weddigen too much while the *U-9* was on the surface; there would be landmarks once he got in coastal waters again, and there were other navigational aids. But when submerged, when the dark waters had closed over the lens of the periscope, he would have no idea of his direction. However, the thought of abandoning his patrol and returning to base never entered his mind. He brought the *U-9* round so that the westerly wind struck her starboard beam and he occasionally checked his course by the North star seen between fleeting clumps of cloud.

Next morning, 21 September, rolling heavily in a beam sea, the *U-9* had the low Dutch coast on her port bow. Weddigen changed course to keep parallel with it. The sea moderated during the day, and by evening the lookout could see the lights of The Hague. Weddigen decided to remain where he was for the night and to proceed toward Ostend at daylight. He dived, intending to spend the night on the bottom, expending neither fuel nor battery power, while the crew rested. But the U-boat kept bumping so heavily, even at her maximum depth of one hundred feet, that Weddigen was obliged to bring her back to the blustering surface for fear of damage.

There she began to ride out the night; until Weddigen, in the conning tower with another man on watch, suddenly gave the order 'Dive, dive!' The two came tumbling down to the control room, and Weddigen briefly announced that some blacked-out destroyers were speeding in their direction. Then the crew heard the thrumming of propellers overhead, gradually fading away. Weddigen decided to stay submerged after all, and the *U-9* glided slowly along a few fathoms down, conserving as much as possible of her precious electrical energy.

Soon after daybreak her broomstick of a periscope poked above the surface and a minute later her conning tower came surging up. Two men ran aft and hoisted the exhaust stack, and the engines took up their dual task of driving the vessel and recharging the batteries. Weddigen and his Number One scanned the horizon through their binoculars; except for a few Dutch fishing-boats to landward, the sea was empty. The wind had dropped, the sky was clear and visibility was very good. Weddigen went below to have breakfast, leaving Speiss on watch.

A few minutes later the captain heard the other's urgent voice resounding down the speaking-tube. 'Captain to the bridge! Diving stations!'

Weddigen bounded up to the conning tower, his mouth still full of food. Speiss pointed and Weddigen took a quick look through his glasses. The line of the horizon was broken by a roll of dark smoke and the mast of a warship. Weddigen gave a grim smile and, seeing that the exhaust stack was already unrigged, ordered 'Dive, dive!'

The *U-9* had been on the surface for less than an hour; the batteries were not yet fully charged and the foul air inside the submarine had not been entirely cleared when Weddigen headed her towards the enemy at periscope depth. His eye to the eyepiece, grasping the handles with both hands and swinging them slightly, he announced that he could make out three four-funnel warships steaming towards him. A few minutes later he identified them as 'three cruisers of the *Birmingham* class'.

'Prepare all tubes for firing!'

The U-boat was sliding towards the cruisers at six knots, the range was closing rapidly, and Weddigen put up his scope less often and for shorter periods. He knew that each time it broke the surface it threw up a long feather of spray which would reveal his presence to an alert lookout. There were many other matters on his mind – not only calculations of course and speed and the tactics of attack but also the problems which might arise after the firing of a torpedo. The sudden loss of weight forward might bring the *U-9* up into full view of the enemy. The explosion might damage her own bow – it was known that the U-boat which had sunk the *Pathfinder* had been severely jarred by the detonation, although the torpedo had been fired at a range of well over a thousand yards. Weddigen was closing the leading cruiser, reducing the range to not much more than five hundred yards to be sure of a hit.

'We are on the enemy,' said Weddigen, his voice loud in the tense silence of the control room. 'As soon as we fire, take her down to fifty feet and hold her there.'

For some time a squadron of elderly armoured cruisers of 12,000 tons had been patrolling the Dogger Bank and the Dutch coast in support of the destroyers operating out of Harwich; but the recent bad weather had forced the destroyers to return to harbour. The old cruisers were well aware of their exposed situation if any German battleships appeared on the scene. This was their chief concern. None of their officers was thinking of U-boats; in seven weeks of war, not a single enemy submarine had even been sighted. The *Aboukir, Hogue* and *Cressy* were steaming in line abreast about two miles apart and at barely ten knots. The *Aboukir,* slightly in advance of her two sister-ships, was on a straight course at a steady speed – presenting the easiest possible target for an enemy torpedo.

Suddenly the *Aboukir* was checked by an explosion amidships and began to sink by the stern. Clouds of dark smoke billowed from her four funnels and groups of white-clad figures started to lower the boats. Then came a flash of flame, and the stricken cruiser began to settle more rapidly, listing to starboard.

The *Cressy* and the *Hogue*, their captains thinking that their consort had struck a mine, closed the sinking ship to pick up survivors. The *Hogue* even stopped when she reached the scene and calmly lowered her boats. At that moment the *Aboukir* slid stern first beneath the waters, leaving a litter of floating wreckage and a few dozen heads bobbing in the sea.

The *U-9* had been neither drawn to the surface nor flung about by the force of the explosion. Weddigen brought her up to periscope depth again to see the effect of his attack, then manoeuvred to fire at the stopped cruiser. Speiss saw to the reloading of the bow tube, while the CPO helped keep the little submarine level by the use of all available men; his orders of 'All hands aft', followed later by 'All hands forward', caused a rush of sweating, panting men from one end of the boat to the other.

Weddigen fired both his bow torpedoes at the sitting target from a distance of only three hundred yards. The *Hogue*, though mortally damaged, remained on an even keel; but five minutes later her quarter-deck was awash. She began to roll over as her crew abandoned ship.

The *Cressy* made no attempt to save herself even now; she remained circling the vast area of wreckage and lifeboats, picking up survivors. It was magnificent but not war.

However, the *U-9*'s batteries were almost discharged and the air was foul with sweat and oil. Weddigen was pushing his boat and his crew to their limits as he circled to fire his stern torpedoes at the remaining cruiser, going in for the final kill. But this time the periscope was sighted and a gun flashed on the cruiser's forward deck. The water churned under her stern as she tried to get up power to ram the U-boat. One torpedo missed her stern by twenty feet but the other struck her aft on the starboard side. For the fourth time the *U-9* crew heard the hollow boom of a torpedo hit, and another cheer rang through her narrow hull.

When Weddigen looked again through the periscope he saw the cruiser listing to starboard and her boats being lowered. She did not seem badly damaged, so he fired his last remaining torpedo and hit the cruiser plump in the middle of her starboard side. Less than two hours after the *U-9* had stolen towards the three proud cruisers, the last of them gave her death roll and vanished with a rush and a rumble.

The *U-9* crept away from the scene on the last dregs of her battery power. Her crew were well aware that destroyers must have been alerted by radio when the second and third torpedoes struck and that revenging ships were on their way. With no torpedoes left, no armament, and her batteries run down, the *U-9* was helpless. Flight on the surface, back to base, was her only hope. She rose streaming, rigged her exhaust stack, and chugged off to the north-west; then, when out of sight of the boatloads of survivors, she turned eastward.

That evening she only just escaped being rammed by an enemy destroyer and was forced to remain all night on the muddy bottom of the North Sea, being still without enough battery power to proceed submerged.

On the morning of 23 September the *U-9* was off the mouth of the Ems and Weddigen radioed his triumphant report. It was picked up by a German minelayer off Wilhelmshaven and relayed to Naval HQ: 'The *U-9* has sunk with six torpedoes, between 06.00 and 09.00 hours on 22 September, three British warships, probably armoured cruisers of the Third Squadron.'

It was a fact that Weddigen and his crew of twenty-five had sent 36,000 tons of fighting ships to the bottom and taken the lives of nearly 1,400 officers and ratings. The submarine had come of age.

2 Submarine versus an Army, May–December 1915

During the night of 19 May 1915 a British submarine was attempting the dangerous and almost impossible feat of passing through the Dardanelles into the Sea of Marmara. The *E-11*, Lieutenant-Commander Martin Nasmith, was a diesel-engined boat, had five torpedo-tubes and carried a spare 'fish' for each. She was slightly larger then the *U-9*, was faster by a knot or two both on the surface and submerged, and had a crew of twenty-eight. Nasmith had to make a submerged passage of about thirty-five miles, and if he proceeded at maximum speed he would drain all the power from the batteries long before reaching the Sea of Marmara; but if he proceeded at an economical cruising speed of four or five knots he would make very slow headway against the adverse current of two to three knots, which increased to four knots in the Narrows, halfway along the Dardanelles. The passage would take about twenty hours, which was almost the limit of the *E-11*'s underwater endurance. And that was not the only hazard. There were enemy minefields and anti-submarine wire nets to negotiate; the Straits were constantly patrolled by Turkish gunboats, and both shores were lined with enemy searchlights and gun-batteries keeping a vigilant lookout for even a periscope poking above the waters.

It was most essential for an Allied submarine to be operating in the Sea of Marmara. Three weeks earlier, on 25 April, the ill-fated Gallipoli campaign had begun; Allied troops had clawed their way ashore at the entrance to the Dardanelles, on the European side, but strong Turkish resistance was keeping them pinned down close to the beaches. The one way of reducing the pressure was by harrying the Turkish lines of communication from Constantinople. These stretched for 130 miles across the Sea of Marmara; the alternative line would be 160 miles by railway and then one hundred miles over roads little better than mule-tracks. If Turkish shipping could be seriously interfered with, the enemy would have grave supply problems. In 1915 aircraft were inadequate for the purpose. Surface warships had already tried to force the Dardanelles and been repulsed with heavy losses, an outcome which had led to the decision to land troops. There remained the new and untried weapon, the submarine.

By 19 May five attempts had already been made by submarines to get through the narrow straits into the Sea of Marmara. The first, the *E-15* (one of the 'overseas' class), had been swept ashore by one of the contrary under-currents which made navigation in the straits so difficult for submarines, and she was shot up by a Turkish battery; the survivors were taken prisoner, and two British picket-boats made a courageous dash to torpedo and destroy the remains of the *E-15*, thus preventing the enemy from gaining any information from her. The second submarine, the Australian *AE-2*, had succeeded in reaching the Sea of Marmara, but two days later had fallen victim to a Turkish torpedo-boat. Then two French submarines had attempted the passage, but neither got through the Dardanelles. The fifth submarine, the *E-14*, had been successful; she had entered the Marmara on 28 April and in three weeks had so terrorized shipping that it was difficult to find a vessel to attack. She had damaged two large transports and a gunboat, but her chief effect was psychological; the reports of her presence were enough to keep vessels in harbour. The help this gave to the hard-pressed Allied forces in their precarious beachhead on the Gallipoli peninsula was incalculable.

When the *E-14* had fired all her torpedoes the crew made good use of the few rifles and revolvers on board, scaring the life out of any small vessel that came their way. At one point the captain, Lieutenant-Commander Boyle, found the view through his periscope suddenly blotted out; he put up the other one and saw a Turkish fisherman leaning out of his boat and grasping the glass of the first periscope. When Boyle lowered it he almost dragged the Turk out of his boat, so longingly did he hang on to it. This little encounter grew into a story about a Turkish fisherman having hung his fez on a periscope and so blinded the submarine.

On 17 May Rear-Admiral de Robeck, the commander of the Allied naval force based at Tenedos, an island some fifteen miles off the entrance to the Dardanelles, recalled the *E-14* by wireless. Boyle found the passage down the Dardanelles comparatively easy, so he said, as he had the strong current in his favour. He was awarded the VC and given accelerated promotion to Commander.

A day after his return, Nasmith and the *E-11* were on the way to replace and emulate him and his crew. Nasmith had been commanding submarines for the past ten years and been captain of the *E-11* since the beginning of the war. But he and his crew had been out of luck so far. In October 1914 they had failed to get through into the Baltic, a most hazardous undertaking; each time the *E-11* surfaced to charge the batteries she had been forced to dive to avoid destruction by enemy destroyers, and was eventually obliged to return to Harwich with engine trouble. In December, while in the Heligoland Bight, Nasmith had sighted the German battle-cruisers returning from their bombardment of East coast towns; although he manoeuvred with skill and daring, he had failed to bag one. Now he and his crew were determined to accomplish the task set them.

Nasmith had met Boyle at dinner with Admiral de Robeck only a few hours before sailing and had learnt all he could about the defences and obstructions in the Dardanelles and conditions in the Sea of Marmara. That night he kept the *E-11* on the surface until he reached the first minefield, as Boyle had done, then took her down to eighty feet. When nearing the Narrows he came up to periscope depth and was immediately fired at; down he went again, and soon the crew heard the rasping of mooring cables along the hull as the submarine passed under another minefield. Benefiting from Boyle's experience, Nasmith increased speed to charge through the wire net at Nagaraa Point. Just round the Point was a shallow bay often used as an anchorage by big ships; from there, guns could support the land batteries firing on the Allied beachheads. Nasmith poked his periscope above the surface, hopefully, and found he had come up among some destroyers; one tried to ram him. The *E-11* dived, and by 10.00 hours was proceeding slowly up the wider part of the Straits. She was through.

Mid-afternoon found her resting on the bottom of the Sea of Marmara. None of the crew moved more than was necessary; breathing was difficult and unpleasant because of the increasingly foul air. At last came the welcome order, 'Prepare to surface.' The hatch was banged open and sweet clean air surged into the stinking submarine; but hardly had the diesels begun to recharge the batteries than a patrolling Turkish gunboat came speeding across the water. The *E-11* was given no peace until night fell over the Marmara, and then she chugged along on the surface on a north-easterly course while her crew were refreshed and she became again an effective war machine, but alone behind the enemy lines.

Nasmith had decided to begin operations off the entrance to the Bosphorus, hoping that a worthwhile target would emerge. He seized a sailing-dhow and used her to camouflage the *E-11*. His Number One, Lieutenant Guy D'Oyly-Hughes, a tall, slim Irishman in his early twenties, trimmed down the submarine so that only her conning-tower showed, and then the dhow was lashed to it. Thus hidden on one side, Nasmith cruised around looking for enemy ships.

This originality was typical of the man. Earlier in the war, while in his 'billet' in the Heligoland Bight, he had saved the pilots of three seaplanes returning from a raid on the Zeppelin sheds at Cuxhaven. They had run out of fuel and came down on the sea. As the *E-11* was about to pick up the pilots, a Zeppelin was seen approaching. Nasmith took off his cap and waved to the crew. The Zeppelin hesitated to drop its bombs – was this a German submarine taking the British pilots prisoner? While the airship was turning to come back for a closer look, Nasmith had taken the last pilot aboard, leapt after him down the conning-tower, slammed the hatch shut and sounded the klaxon. The *E-11* dived fast, just before two bombs dropped by the infuriated crew of the Zeppelin exploded harmlessly on the surface above.

However, Nasmith's ruse this time proved of no avail, for the Turks seemed to have altogether abandoned their sea communications. The ill-luck which had been dogging the *E-11* since the beginning of the war appeared to have accompanied her all the way to Turkish waters. But on the morning of the third day in the Sea of Marmara, while lying off Oxia Island in a flat calm, Nasmith saw a large transport heading for Constantinople. He gave chase, and found himself almost face to face with a Turkish gunboat. He fired a torpedo and scored a hit – the *E-11*'s luck had changed. The enemy crew, opening fire with their vessel sinking under them, nevertheless shot a piece out of one of *E-11*'s periscopes. Nasmith retired to

Kalolimno Island, some twenty-five miles to the south-west, and there repaired the periscope while the crew bathed.

Next day, while at periscope depth off Constantinople, Nasmith sighted a small steamer. He surfaced and signalled to her to stop. She took no notice, until a few rounds from a rifle caused a change of mind. Nasmith ordered the crew to abandon ship and put D'Oyly-Hughes on board with a demolition party. He found she was carry guns and ammunition, and when he and his party had returned to the *E-11* and the charge was fired, the steamer blew up amidst a column of smoke and flame. There had been an American journalist on board, and before he took to the boats with the crew D'Oyly-Hughes had shouted a few questions to him across several yards of water. The American, being a neutral, had given non-committal answers. D'Oyly-Hughes had gathered that his name was 'Swing', but when writing up the log that evening thought this somewhat inadequate and with Irish inventiveness put: 'An American gentleman appeared on the upper deck and informed us that his name was Silas Q. Swing of the *Chicago Sun*, and that he was pleased to make our acquaintance.' The journalist was actually Raymond Gram Swing, then working for the *Chicago Daily News*, who later made a name for himself in broadcasting.

Soon after blowing up the ammunition ship, Nasmith chased a deeply-laden steamer which succeeded in reaching the little port of Rodosto, on the northern shore. Nasmith went in after her, submerged in water so shallow that as the *E-11* bumped along the bottom her periscope standards were showing above the water. This attracted some hot but inaccurate rifle fire. Nasmith fired a torpedo, taking the chance of it hitting the sea-bed right in front of the *E-11*'s bows. It struck the steamer amidships and she erupted into smoke and flame.

While the *E-11* was withdrawing into deeper water,

Nasmith sighted a paddle-steamer whose decks were piled high with rolls of barbed-wire. He surfaced, and the Turkish vessel ran herself ashore. Nasmith again went into shallow water and was preparing to send off a boarding party when some cavalry came galloping along the shore, dismounted and opened fire. Their bullets were coming uncomfortably close, so Nasmith dived and fired a torpedo; it missed the steamer – a difficult target, being stern-on – and exploded on the beach. Thus ended the first and probably the only engagement between cavalry and a submarine.

On the following day, 25 May, the *E-11* made history. Early in the morning Nasmith dived off Constantinople and daringly took her right into the Bosphorus until, through the periscope, he could see up the Golden Horn. He was the first enemy to enter Constantinople harbour for some five hundred years. And he proceeded to better this exploit by destroying a large transport tied up at the naval arsenal. The first torpedo missed but the second hit the target. Nasmith took a photograph of the transport on fire by putting a camera to the eye-piece of the periscope. Then he got the hell out of it, diving to eighty feet and heading back to the Sea of Marmara, leaving Constantinople in a state of panic with shops closing and all troops being hastily disembarked from their transports.

A few days later the *E-11* sank another large supply ship and attacked one more, but the torpedo just missed. Nasmith calmly recovered it for future use, himself performing the dangerous task of removing the firing-pistol; he had set his torpedoes to float after their run, in order to eke out his supply. When he returned to the Dardanelles on his way back to base on 7 June he still had two torpedoes left, and he was hoping to use them on the warships lying in Nagara bay. There were none, he found, so he took *E-11* back up the Straits and torpedoed a large transport he had passed on the way down. Then he turned again and continued the homeward run. When past the minefields in the Narrows he rose to periscope depth to have a look round.

'Anything interesting to see, sir?' asked his Number One.

'No, only the coast,' Nasmith calmly replied. Within a few feet of the periscope there was in fact a weed-covered mine, being towed along close above the hull. Its mooring wire must have got caught in one of the hydroplanes.

Nasmith kept this unpleasant news to himself; there was no point in alarming the crew yet. 'Take her down to ninety feet, coxswain,' he ordered, and then thought how to get rid of the mine.

When the *E-11* was nearing the entrance to the Dardanelles Nasmith ordered full speed astern and the after main ballast-tanks to be blown. The submarine broke surface at an angle, and as she gathered stern-way the mine-mooring slid clear of the hydroplanes.

So ended a patrol of twenty days during which the *E-11* had disrupted enemy communications and destroyed a gunboat, two troopships and four supply ships. For this exploit Nasmith was awarded the Victoria Cross.

After a refit in Malta the *E-11* and her crew, still with Nasmith in command, went into the Sea of Marmara for a second time. The *E-14* was already there again, but as the Allied army on Gallipoli was about to mount an offensive it had been decided that the maximum of havoc must be caused to Turkish communications. Since the *E-11* had come out of the Marmara in June there had always been at least one British submarine operating in it, and the Turks had almost abandoned sea transport. Nasmith consequently received orders to harry their land communications as much as possible, and to this end a twelve-pounder had been mounted on the *E-11*'s fore-deck.

The passage up the Dardanelles, which the *E-11* entered

just before daylight on 5 August, was even more difficult and nerve-racking than it had been in May. Other submarines had reported new obstructions, and Nasmith soon ran foul of them. He proceeded on the surface as long as possible, then dived to periscope depth, and a few minutes later he and all the crew felt the bows being forced upwards. A few more feet and the hull would be exposed to the fire of an alert shore battery – and the patrol be over before it began. Nasmith's quick submariner's mind grasped the trouble: something must have fouled his bridge or periscope. He downed periscope and went a few feet lower. The obstruction cleared. He put up his periscope again, swung it to look astern and saw the latest Turkish snare – a line of buoys supporting a wire cable intended to bend periscopes and blind the submarine or to bring her to the surface.

The *E-11* then dived deep to pass under the minefields in the Narrows, and about ten minutes later she was in an even more serious situation. The crew were expecting to hear the rasping of mooring-wires along the hull, but when there came a clanging bump on the starboard bow everyone froze. It came again, amidships. Not a man but realized that it was a mine, one laid specially deep to catch a submarine. The third blow would assuredly destroy them. But after an agonizing wait they realized with infinite relief that the mine had swung clear of the stern. 'Bad egg,' someone nervously remarked; but they had been saved by the fact that it was a mine of the ordinary type with horned detonators pointing upwards to catch the bottoms of surface ships, and the *E-11* had struck its lower part.

Nasmith went deeper still, for the experience was not one to be repeated. However, the *E-11* had not finished with the new obstructions. A wire-mesh net had been reported just above Nagara Point, and when the navigator, Lieutenant Robert Brown, judged that the *E-11* was approaching the obstacle

Nasmith took her down to 110 feet and rushed at it, hoping to pass under it. But the net had been extended. The *E-11* was checked and thrown upwards some twenty feet. Men grabbed at pipes and valves to save themselves from falling. Nasmith did the only thing possible. 'Full speed ahead!' The whine of the motors rose to a high pitch, there came the twanging of parting wires, and suddenly the *E-11* was through.

Around the Point was the anchorage where Turkish warships sometimes lay. Nasmith felt it time to go over to the offensive. To his disappointment there were no battleships to torpedo, but there was a large transport; and a few minutes later she was developing a rapid list to port while the *E-11* was moving up the Straits at a depth of thirty feet, her account for this patrol already opened.

By mid-afternoon the *E-11* was far enough into the Sea of Marmara to surface to recharge her batteries. But Turkish patrol boats had obviously been alerted that an enemy submarine had passed through the Dardanelles, for time and again Nasmith was forced to dive hurriedly to escape their unwelcome attentions. It was the May experience all over again; the crew had to sweat it out until nightfall, and then the submarine was able to chug along on the surface and the men came up top a few at a time to feel and breath the refreshing night air. Soon after dawn a Turkish seaplane almost put paid to the intruder; it came swooping down with the rising sun behind it, engines throttled back, and dropped two bombs before the *E-11* could begin to submerge. They straddled the bow some fifty yards apart, but no damage was done.

Later that morning Nasmith made his rendezvous with the *E-14,* still commanded by Boyle. While lookouts on the bridge of each submarine constantly swept the enemy sea and sky through their binoculars, the two captains exchanged news and agreed on tactics for one of the most curious amphibian operations in history. Boyle knew of a strip of coast near

Dolan Aslan where the one road to Gallipoli ran along by the shore, and on the morning of 7 August both submarines were there lying in wait at periscope depth, the crews at surfacing stations.

'Down periscope! Surface!' Nasmith had seen a column of troops marching along the road.

The gun's crew were out of the hatch while the foredeck was still a-swirl with water. The first shell hit the hillside just above the road; the second fell among the troops, and they scattered into the fields and scrub. For nearly an hour the *E-11*'s twelve-pounder stopped all movement along the road to Gallipoli. And this was repeated twice in the afternoon, the actions being tersely entered in the log:

13.10 hours. Large column observed on road to Gallipoli, marching at high speed. Opened fire, but failed to stop progress of column, although a large number of dead and wounded appeared to be left alongside the road. This column was under fire for about half-an-hour, when we were forced to dive by shore guns.

15.20 hours. Rose to the surface and opened fire at a considerable body of troops, apparently resting. They immediately dispersed, and subsequently opened a well-directed fire with a field-gun. Dived.

The *E-14*, too, had been causing much hindrance further along the coast, though as she had only a six-pounder the damage was less. Then she also came under fire from field-guns and wisely withdrew from the scene.

Those field-guns were badly needed by the Turks for use against the Allied offensive, and it must have been particularly galling to retain them to protect infantry being pinned down by a submarine.

Nasmith reckoned that the Turks would be using all available means to rush reinforcements and supplies to the peninsula, so he spent that night patrolling the western end of the Sea of Marmara. He had turned in, leaving D'Oyly-Hughes on watch, but was alert in a moment when, soon after four in the morning, there came a shout of 'Captain to the bridge!' A smudge of black smoke on the eastern horizon indicated a big ship speeding his way. He dived, and lay in wait with his crew at action stations. Twenty minutes later he fired a bow torpedo at the Turkish battleship *Hairedin Barbarossa* and hit her amidships. A sheet of flame shot up, and she slowed down; the escorting destroyer heeled over and doubled back, and Nasmith took swift evading action. When he rose ten minutes later to have a brief look round through the periscope he saw the *Barbarossa* listing dangerously to starboard and creeping towards the coast. A few minutes afterwards she blew up and sank. The *E-11*'s crew were jubilant, and even the austere Nasmith gave a smile of satisfaction.

The *E-14* was actively engaged, too, that morning. Nasmith received a radio message from her: a 5,000-ton troopship that she had torpedoed had been beached, and she was shelling the vessel; the assistance of the *E-11*'s bigger gun would be appreciated. Nasmith headed up the coast at fifteen knots and joined in the firing. The transport, abandoned by crew and troops, was soon burning briskly. Then came disaster. The *E-11*'s gun had fired a dozen rounds when the gunlayer was suddenly thrown backwards into the sea; he was fished out little the worse, but the gun was in a bad way. The upper part of the mounting had been fractured by the recoil, and the wonder was that the weapon had not followed the gunlayer overboard. Without a gun, the *E-11* could not carry out her mission of harassing land communications.

Nasmith sent for Chief Engine-room Artificer Allen, who examined the damaged metal and grunted in a non-committal way, as Chief ERAs tend to do. Then the gun was lashed securely so that the *E-11* could submerge if necessary and Nasmith set course for a little frequented part of the Sea of Marmara. There Allen and his team succeeded in repairing the gun. The job might not have been approved by a naval dockyard – for one thing, the gun-mounting was a foot or so lower and in a moment of excitement it was possible for the *E-11* to shell and sink herself – but the twelve-pounder was an effective weapon again.

Nasmith searched in vain for another worthwhile target for his precious torpedoes, but the Turks seemed reduced to sending a trickle of material in sailing dhows. Nasmith's method of dealing with these was to round up half-a-dozen, order the crews of five into the sixth and sent it into the nearest port, then lash the five craft together and set them alight. This saved explosives, and the columns of smoke were reminders that the Marmara was no longer a Turkish sea.

Nasmith planned his cruising so that every other night he was at the western end of the Marmara and able to report by radio and receive orders from a communications ship at the other end of the Dardanelles. The *E-14* was relieved by the *E-2* and Nasmith was informed that the latter was bringing him a fresh supply of ammunition and explosives. He duly made the rendezvous with Lieutenant-Commander Stocks, the captain of the *E-2*, and when the essential work had been done each crew mustered on the conning-tower and foredeck and, one hundred miles behind the enemy lines, souvenir photographs were taken. *E-11*'s crew looked a bunch of bearded pirates by then; only their captain stood out – he still shaved once a day as a matter of principle.

Ten days after entering the Marmara he repeated his exploit of diving into the Bosphorus and torpedoing a ship in Constantinople harbour, this time a collier about to unload several thousand tons of coal. Then he went trainhunting in the Gulf of Ismid, at the far eastern end of the Marmara. Here the high mountains came down to the sea, and for nearly thirty miles the railway line from Baghdad to Constantinople – a vital link in the Turkish communications – ran close to the shore. Nasmith's chief objective was an iron viaduct a quarter-of-a-mile long. He surfaced about four hundred yards off shore and at once opened up with the twelve-pounder. But before the bombardment had any effect on the viaduct, first one and then another field-gun began to return the fire. A shot sprayed the submarine's stern; Nasmith quickly decided that his position was untenable. 'Cease firing! Clear the bridge! Stand by to dive!' He followed the last gunner down the hatch, slammed the lid shut and rammed home the safety clips. Fortunately the water was deep even close inshore; for many minutes after the *E-11* had disappeared from the sight of the Turkish gunners her crew could hear the angry slap of shells hitting the water.

It was obvious that a long bombardment of the viaduct would not be possible, and so one of the most daring single-handed exploits of the First World War was planned and put into operation. But first Nasmith took his command away to the other end of the Marmara and spent four days chasing and burning dhows and shelling the coastal road, hoping that things would quieten down a bit in the Gulf of Ismid.

In the dark early hours of 21 August the *E-11* was back there again, trimmed down to show as little of herself as possible while nosing in towards the cliff-lined shore. Two of the crew lowered a raft into the water; on it were D'Oyly-Hughes's uniform, a sixteen-pound tin of guncotton, a whistle, a revolver and ammunition, and a sharp bayonet. Then D'Oyly-Hughes (whose idea this was) slipped into the water and swam for the shore pushing the raft in front of him. The *E-11* moved slowly out to sea and lay to, waiting to pick up her Number One when he returned from his mission,

36

which was to blow up the viaduct if he found it unguarded, otherwise to damage the permanent way where he could.

D'Oyly-Hughes had some difficulty in finding a place to get ashore; he swam with the raft several hundred yards westward before coming to cliffs that were scalable. There he landed, quickly got into his uniform and climbed inland. The railway line must have taken a bend not visible from the sea, for he stumbled and scrambled in the dark for half-an-hour before he came to it. He followed it along towards the viaduct, but soon heard voices; creeping forward, he saw three sentries sitting on the embankment and chatting. He would have to make a wide detour to pass them unseen and reconnoitre as far as the viaduct, and time was of the essence; it was not long before dawn. He hid his explosives so that he could move fast, then cut across country; it was not easy to keep a sense of direction, for there were several small farmhouses in the area and these had to be avoided. As it was, on climbing a low wall which he thought divided two fields, he landed in the middle of a poultry yard and set up a terrific squawking. But no alarm was raised, and soon afterwards he made out the high outline of the viaduct – and heard great activity around it. Creeping closer, he saw a camp-fire burning, men with lanterns and others hammering at the railway line. Work was still going on at repairing the damage done by the *E-11*'s gun, and there was obviously no chance of approaching and blowing the viaduct.

D'Oyly-Hughes retraced his steps, carefully avoiding the poultry yard. He recovered his explosives and searched for a good place to use them. A small culvert offered the chance of doing most damage, but it was not far from the three soldiers guarding the line; and he would have to light his fuse with a percussion device that gave a loud crack. However, the opportunity was too good to miss and he decided on bold action. He packed his sixteen pounds of guncotton into a hole he made in the stonework, lit the fuse, and as the report echoed on the still air he started running down the line in full view of the Turkish soldiers. As he had hoped, the three chased him instead of investigating the cause of the report. He fired a couple of shots at them with his revolver, they stopped to reply with their rifles, and he turned towards the sea. Slithering and stumbling down the rocky slope, he reached the shore and splashed into the water. Just then he heard a thunderous roar behind him and knew he had accomplished his mission.

He swam out to sea some way but there was no sign of the *E-11*. He blew lustily on the whistle which was slung round his neck but no reply came. Then he realized that he was too far west of the place where he had gone ashore, and so even farther from where the submarine would be waiting for him. He was too exhausted to swim along the coast, fully clothed as he was; there was nothing for it but to return to the shore and work his way along, hoping that the Turkish soldiers were looking for him elsewhere. After covering about half-a-mile he decided that the sea was the safer place, for by this time day was breaking, and he swam out to a small rocky point; there he floated and blew his whistle again. The reply was a rattle of rifle fire.

The Turks, however, were firing at the submarine. Nasmith and his crew knew that D'Oyly-Hughes had blown something up, for several chunks of masonry had fallen on the submarine as she moved in to look for him. Nasmith was getting very anxious about him; then his whistle was heard and a few minutes later eager hands were hauling him back on board.

Three nights later the *E-11* was proceeding submerged down the Dardanelles. Nasmith had received a signal that an Allied air patrol had sighted four large transports anchored above the Narrows, evidently landing supplies for the Turkish forces on the peninsula. At seven in the morning Nasmith had the ships in sight, two on either side of the Straits; and as he took a rapid look round, his arms crooked over the handles of the periscope and his feet shuffling round the well-worn patch of deck, he saw too that the supply ships were well screened by a number of craft including a gunboat and a destroyer. In order to attack the supply ships he would have to get this screening force out of the way. Fortunately he still had five torpedoes left; some had been recovered after being fired and missing their mark. One was used against the gunboat, but it ran under her and exploded among some small craft tied up along the bank. At once a submarine hunt was on. All the Turkish vessels of the screening force headed up-channel, drawn by frequent, tantalizing glimpses of the *E-11*'s periscope and even the top of her conning-tower. When Nasmith had enticed them well away from the supply ships he dived deep and turned back, straight under the pursuing surface force. He rose to periscope depth when abreast of the unguarded ships on the Gallipoli side and bagged them both with a 'right and left' from his bow torpedo-tubes. Then he dived across to the other shore, hit and sank the third supply ship, and with his last torpedo damaged the remaining ship as she was getting under way, and she beached herself.

Nasmith succeeded in taking the *E-11* back to the Marmara, shooting up the railway, troop concentrations on the coastal road and supply dumps with his twelve-pounder, and destroying a number of dhows carrying war material. On 3 September Nasmith received his recall signal. He had been warned by Stocks that the Turks had strung a new, stronger underwater net across the Narrows, so he charged it at full speed at a depth of eighty feet, aided by the current. D'Oyly-Hughes was stationed in the conning-tower with the deadlights up, hoping to see the net through the thick glass and learn something of its construction. The *E-11* burst through the net and returned safely to base bringing much valuable information including the fact that the new net was made of two-and-a-half inch wire and had ten-foot meshes.

The day after the *E-11* returned from her highly successful twenty-nine-day patrol, the *E-7* sailed to replace her in the Marmara but got entangled in the net; the captain was forced to surface and surrender, after a time-fuse had been fired to blow up the boat. This left the *E-2* alone in the Marmara for a time. One morning before dawn her Number One, Lieutenant Lyon, went ashore as D'Oyly-Hughes had done, with gun-cotton, knife and revolver, to blow a railway bridge on the line from Constantinople to Rodosto. But he was never heard of again. And nothing was learnt about his fate even when the Turkish records became available after the war.

The *E-2* was relieved on 16 September, and for the next couple of months there were usually two British submarines operating in the Marmara. In early November Nasmith and the *E-11* were back there again. And again they terrorized the Turks, shelling trains and sinking ships, including a destroyer. They were joined by their old companion the *E-2* on 10 December, and Nasmith learnt from Stocks that the Turks had laid more net defences in the Dardanelles since his own passage a month earlier. The two submarines went their separate ways, having arranged to meet again a week later. Nasmith haunted the approaches to Constantinople and took the *E-11* into the Bosphorus for a third time, and sank a large steamer crossing from the Golden Horn.

There was now a third submarine in the Marmara – a German which had been transported overland in sections and assembled at Constantinople. In October this submarine, the *UB-14,* had torpedoed and sunk the British *E-20,* and now she almost brought the *E-11*'s glorious career to a close. When Nasmith went to keep his rendezvous with the *E-2* he narrowly escaped being torpedoed by the German. He signalled the enemy presence to Stocks, who sighted her two days later and tried to ram her, but she dived and escaped.

Nasmith was recalled on 23 December and passed successfully down the Dardanelles. The *E-11*'s third patrol had been her longest and a record – forty-seven days, during which she accounted for one destroyer, eleven steamers and thirty-five sailing vessels. Altogether Nasmith and his gallant crew spent ninety-six days in the hostile Marmara and put paid to one hundred and one enemy vessels of all kinds.

But it was all in vain, for soon afterwards the Gallipoli evacuation was completed.

3 Caught up in a Revolution, 1917-8

While the *E-11* and other submarines were being aggressive against the Turks in the Sea of Marmara, several E-class boats were actively engaged against the Germans in the Baltic. This sea was the only area in which the German navy could carry out exercises, without which a fleet soon loses its efficiency; and across the Baltic went the iron-ore that Germany imported from Scandinavia to meet the ever-increasing demands of her armament factories.

Whereas submarines had to make that difficult and dangerous passage of the Dardanelles to enter and leave the Marmara, those operating in the Baltic stayed in – once they had got in – and were based on Russian ports, chiefly Reval in the Gulf of Finland. Supplies and spare parts reached them by the sea route to Archangel and then overland. And they came under the orders of Admiral von Essen, the Russian naval C-in-C, who seemed to think that their main task was the protection of the Imperial Russian Navy from German raids.

The British crews and their captains had difficulties and problems enough. There was the handicap of trying to cooperate with an inefficient and antiquated navy lacking an offensive spirit and of working with people whose language they did not understand. When at sea they were unable to adopt the free-wheeling tactics of Nasmith and others. Unlike the Sea of

Marmara, the Baltic was mined; it was patrolled by highly efficient German anti-submarine vessels; the Scandinavian countries were neutral and their territorial waters had to be avoided – though the Germans did not respect these neutral waters; and in winter much of the sea was frozen over, creating conditions of which the small and somewhat primitive submarines had little or no experience.

In the summer of 1915 there were only two British submarines operating in the Baltic: the *E-1* and the *E-9*, commanded respectively by Lieutenant-Commanders Laurence and Horton [who became Flag Officer Submarines during the Second World War]. Between them, however, they had sunk or damaged a number of German ships and their patrols had deterred the Germans from carrying out a combined operation to occupy the Gulf of Finland. In fact it would be no exaggeration to say that but for the activities of the *E-1* and *E-9* the Germans might well have been in St Petersburg by the end of that summer.

Still, the Russians became greatly alarmed at the development of the German offensive against Riga and other of their west-coast ports, and they asked for an increase in the number of British submarines in the Baltic. So on 15 August 1915 the *E-8* and *E-13* left Harwich to join their sister submarines. Three nights later the *E-8*, having passed through the Skagerrack and round the Skaw, was trying to negotiate the Sound, literally crawling along the bottom of those shallow and narrow waters. Her captain, Lieutenant-Commander Goodhart, found that it was like trying to get through a crowded harbour without being seen. There were vessels everywhere, all showing confusing lights, and between Copenhagen and Malmo both shores were lit up. It was impossible to tell friend and neutral from foe; there was not enough sea room to avoid curious or dangerous craft, and not enough depth of water to get underneath them. At one point the *E-8* was caught in the searchlight of a torpedo-boat Goodhart dived, and the submarine hit the bottom hard at nineteen feet, bounced up and then struck the bottom again – this time at fourteen feet. At that depth the periscope standards were above water. The submarine scraped along, edging past a German destroyer without being spotted. One hard bump tore all the blades off the starboard propeller. But eventually slightly deeper water was reached; a few hours later Goodhart surfaced, only to dive hastily to avoid a destroyer. By then, mid-morning, the batteries were very low. The *E-8* lay on the bottom for the rest of the day. When darkness fell Goodhart made several attempts to surface but, like Nasmith the previous year, he was repeatedly 'put down' by patrol vessels before he could begin to recharge the batteries. Eventually, about midnight, he did manage to lie on the surface for a couple of hours. But dawn comes very early in the Baltic in summer, and he had to dive again before the batteries were fully charged and the crew refreshed. However, by sheer persistence he succeeded in reaching the entrance to the Gulf of Finland, where he was met by the *E-9* and shepherded to Reval.

It had taken the *E-8* almost a week, but the *E-13* never arrived at all. She passed through the Sound a few hours later than the *E-8*, but then her compass failed, and before this was detected she ran aground on the Saltholm sandbank, in Danish territorial waters. Her captain and crew made desperate efforts to get her off but were still there at daybreak. A Danish gunboat approached and informed Lieutenant-Commander Layton that, in accordance with International Law, he and his crew would be interned if they failed to get away within twenty-four hours. At about 09.00 hours two German destroyers appeared on the scene, and when the leading ship was within half-a-mile of the helpless *E-13* she fired a torpedo; it hit the bottom close to the submarine but did no damage. Then, despite the presence of the Danish gunboat and a guardship, the Germans opened fire on the defenceless submarine at three hundred yards' range. She was hit repeatedly by four-inch shells and caught fire. Layton gave the order to abandon ship, and as the crew swam for the shore or the Danish vessels they were machine-gunned by the Germans. Fifteen were killed, and the others were saved only by the Danish vessels steaming between them and the German destroyer and picking them up.

The survivors were interned and well treated by the Danes, but after three weeks Lieutenant-Commander Layton withdrew his parole and escaped to Sweden; from there he eventually got back to England, eager to have his revenge on the Germans.

The third British submarine in the Baltic, the *E-1*, had already avenged the *E-13* to some extent, even while the atrocity was being committed.

The German High Command had mounted a combined operation to turn the flank of the Russian army by capturing Riga, and to this end the Baltic squadron of the German navy was reinforced by units of the High Sea Fleet. On 19 August a large force sailed from Kiel and Danzig to attack the Gulf of Riga. Vice-Admiral Schmidt was in command of a battle fleet of two battleships, four cruisers and thirty-three destroyers, and in support were eight battleships, three battle-cruisers, five cruisers and a number of destroyers under the command of Vice-Admiral Hipper. So jittery were the Germans because of the activities of the British submarines in the Baltic during the previous months that this armada had been allowed to put to sea only 'provided adequate precautions against loss were taken' – loss by two lone British submarines.

That morning, 19 August, the *E-1* was on patrol south of the entrance to the Gulf of Riga when her captain, Lieutenant-Commander Laurence, sighted some German battle-cruisers steaming in line abreast. Visibility was not very good and the enemy squadron was moving at speed. Laurence man-oeuvred quickly to take up an attacking position and fired a torpedo at the starboard-wing ship, the *Seydlitz*. Before he could fire again he had to dive deep to avoid being rammed by a destroyer which came racing towards him. Then the *E-1* developed engine trouble and later crawled back to her base at Reval.

Her one torpedo had missed the *Seydlitz* but hit the next ship in the line, the *Moltke*. This was enough for Admiral Hipper; although the *Moltke* did not sink, he signalled his entire force to return to Danzig. He had no wish to displease a Kaiser who had as little understanding of sea power as Napoleon.

The *E-1*'s single torpedo thus led to the withdrawal of the naval forces; and without them the German land forces failed to advance against Riga. The whole operation was called off, and was revived only when the Bolshevik Revolution broke out in October 1917.

When Laurence arrived at Reval he was sent for by the Tsar, Nicholas II, who thanked him and said 'You have saved our town of Riga.'

There being no warships to attack, the British submarines were confined to the task of enforcing the blockade. This was not without its excitements and successes, evidenced by one day in the life of the *E-19*, which had replaced the lost *E-13* in the Baltic. On 11 October, soon after 09.00 hours, the *E-19* stopped the *Walter Leonhardt*, bound for Hamburg with a cargo of iron-ore. Lieutenant-Commander Cromie, the *E-19*'s captain, ordered the German crew to abandon ship. They took to the boats in a rough sea; driving rain-squalls almost blotted them out, and they were far from land. Cromie, having due regard for international law and the safety of crews of unarmed merchant-ships, wondered what to do; he had no room for the Germans in his small submarine. Then he saw a steamer on the horizon and chased after her. She was Swedish, and Cromie persuaded her skipper to alter course and take on board the crew of the *Walter Leonhardt*. He then sent a demolition party across, and a little later the ship and her valuable cargo sank to the bottom of the Baltic.

By noon that day the *E-19* was chasing after another German steamer, but when Cromie signalled to her to stop she headed at full speed for the shore and beached herself. When the *E-19* approached, Cromie found that the crew had got ashore and the ship was badly damaged. She was laden with three thousand tons of iron-ore, which could be salvaged, so Cromie tried to tow her off into deeper water where he could sink her; but the *E-19*'s engines were not powerful enough. However, the ship was left filling with water. An hour or so later Cromie stopped the German cargo-ship *Gutrune*, also bound for Hamburg with more than four thousand tons of iron-ore. Again he saw to the safety of the crew by putting them aboard a neutral ship before sinking the *Gutrune* by gunfire – all E-class submarines now carried guns, profiting from the earlier experiences in the Sea of Marmara.

Cromie was finding some advantage from operating in waters much used by neutral shipping. But later in the afternoon he experienced some of the inconveniences too. He sighted two large cargo-ships each on a southerly course and went in pursuit of one of them – the wrong one, for she turned out to be Swedish, the *Nyland*. Cromie's Number One boarded her and examined her papers; she had a cargo of iron-ore consigned to Rotterdam, so it would probably reach the enemy through a neutral country. However, Cromie had enough to contend with already and had no wish to become involved in the intricacies of a Prize Court; he was at war, and the other ship was making full speed towards the horizon. He allowed the *Nyland* to proceed, and dashed after the second vessel. She was a German bound from Stockholm to Nadenheim with a cargo of iron-ore. Cromie sank her, then hailed yet another Swedish ship, bound for Newcastle, and put the German crew aboard her.

The day's work was not yet over for the *E-19*. The light was beginning to fade when she overhauled the German vessel *Nicomedia*, which tried to reach Swedish territorial waters. A shot across her bows from *E-19*'s gun brought her to. She was loaded with seven thousand tons of iron-ore and bound for Hamburg. Cromie ordered the crew into their boats – the coast of Sweden was little more than three miles away – and then the fifth ship of the day was sent to the bottom. Altogether some twenty thousand tons of badly-needed iron-ore had been denied to the enemy, and without causing death or injury to a single non-combatant.

Cromie had done quite right in stopping the *Nyland* and examining her papers. The following day he stopped another Swedish vessel, the *Nike*, and her papers showed that her cargo of iron-ore was destined for the German port of Stettin. This was a very different matter. Cromie promptly arrested her for carrying contraband to the enemy, and put an officer and prize crew on board with orders to take her to Reval. On the way the *E-19*'s officer learnt from the *Nike*'s captain that when he had left Lulea, the Swedish port at the head of the Gulf of Bothnia, there were fifteen German ships loaded with iron-ore and apparently waiting for an escort in order to sail. This information was passed on to the British submarines on patrol in the Baltic. However, the *Nike* created a problem. The Russians had no wish to annoy Sweden, where there was already sympathy enough for Germany; but the *Nike* was a British prize. Eventually a solution was found: the *Nike* was handed over to Russia as a courteous gesture to an Ally, and the Russians then returned her to Sweden.

A week after Cromie's 'day out', the *E-9* continued the good work by sinking four German cargo-ships, probably some of those which had been dallying in the port of Lulea. The last of the four appeared to have a destroyer escort, though she was some distance away; she came cutting decidedly towards the *E-9* when Lieutenant-Commander Horton stopped the German ship and ordered the crew to abandon her. Horton was not sure of the destroyer's nationality, but as she seemed intent on ramming the *E-9* he promptly crash-dived. On coming up to periscope depth he saw the destroyer stopped and picking up the German crew from their boats. He also saw that she was a Swedish destroyer, the *Wale*. So he surfaced, whereupon the destroyer signalled that he was in Swedish territorial waters.

'I make myself six miles from land,' Horton replied.

'I make you five,' signalled the *Wale*.

'Neutral limit is three miles. Please stand clear while I sink this ship.'

The destroyer then stood off, and Horton fired his stern tube at the German ship. She sank within a few minutes.

At this time Lieutenant-Commander Goodhart in the *E-8* was patrolling off the port of Libau, which had been captured by the Germans early that summer. For some days he lay in wait for a vessel to leave or enter, watching destroyers patrolling the harbour entrance and the swept channel through the minefields. On the morning of 23 October his patience was rewarded in a big way. A three-funnel cruiser came steaming out escorted by two destroyers which zigzagged in advance of their charge. Goodhart had a difficult approach to make, for it was a bright sunny day with a calm sea – conditions which were favourable to the enemy for detecting the periscope or the wash of a submarine speeding along at periscope depth. Goodhart reduced speed as the range shortened, taking a quick look through the periscope from time to time. In the briefest of glances he had to take in everything that was happening on the surface. The crew watched his face; his eye was the eye of them all.

'Down periscope. Hard a-starboard. Bring the tubes to the ready.'

Goodhart was manoeuvring to pass astern of the port screening destroyer and run in for a beam shot at the cruiser. The range was down to two thousand yards and the submarine's speed reduced to five knots to lessen the wake.

'Up periscope – slowly!' Goodhart bent to straighten up with it, his eye glued to the eyepiece. The crew at their stations were tense with expectation. Their captain saw the bows of the cruiser coming into his field of vision.

'Fire!'

The submarine gave a sort of hiccough as the torpedo shot out of its tube. The range was thirteen hundred yards, and a minute after firing came the deep boom of an explosion. Goodhart had taken the *E-8* down to fifty feet; ten minutes later he rose to have a quick look round. There was no sign of the cruiser. The destroyers were stopped, picking up survivors. Goodhart concluded that the loss of the cruiser had been attributed to a mine, so he glided away, silent and invisible.

The ship he had sunk was the 9,000-ton *Prinz Adalbert*, the flagship of the German Baltic squadron.

A fortnight later the *E-19*, on her last patrol before winter set in, hit and sank a German light cruiser. Altogether the few British submarines were proving to be the terror of the Baltic. German warships were confined to harbour and even the trials of newly launched ships were postponed. When offensive operations again became possible, in the spring of 1916, it seemed that the British submarines would have to enter enemy harbours in order to attack warships. Indeed, Cromie got tired of patrolling off Memel for days without sighting a single ship; he took the *E-19* in towards the harbour, after telling his crew of the risks involved and getting their wholehearted approval. But the submarine became entangled in a wire net much stronger than any in the Dardanelles, and extricated herself only after hours of struggle. The situation had become so desperate, with electric power almost exhausted, that Cromie destroyed all the secret papers and had explosive charges placed near the torpedoes, preparatory to surfacing and surrendering. But with a last terrific effort the *E-19* had freed herself. . . . Only to be virtually immobilized on her return to base, as were her consorts, by mutiny in the Russian fleet and the setting up of a provisional government.

The Russians continued to treat the British officers and ratings with respect, but when sailors' committees or councils took the place of the old order there was so much confusion and nonsensical arrangements that any effective action against the enemy became almost impossible. The British submarines carried on as long as they could against Germany, but lack of fuel and supplies soon drastically reduced their activities.

This was frustrating enough for the crews, but worse was to follow. At the beginning of 1917 there were seven British submarines in the Baltic – the *E-1, E-8, E-9* and *E-19*, and three of the smaller C-class, which had been sent overland from Archangel – and they were berthed at Reval alongside an old Russian cruiser which served as a depot ship. When the Tsar abdicated and a revolutionary government was set up, the British submarines and their depot ship moved across the Gulf of Finland to Helsingfors (Helsinki) in order to escape to some extent from the effects of the Revolution and with the faint hope of being able to resume hostilities. But this hope faded entirely when the Bolsheviks seized power and sued for peace with Germany.

It was impossible for the submarines to attempt to make the passage out of the Baltic, and orders came for most of their crews to return to England via Archangel. Left behind was a 'care and maintenance party' under Lieutenant Downie, the commander of one of the C-boats, and consisting of one warrant engineer and twenty-two ratings. Cromie, who had spent the long winter months learning Russian, also stayed on as a sort of provisional naval attaché to the provisional government, with the rank of captain.

The little party of submariners settled to the task of keeping the seven submarines and the stock of torpedoes in efficient order. At the same time the eventuality of being suddenly forced to destroy them all had to be provided for; the best that could be done with the limited means available was to connect some alarm-clocks to an electrical demolition circuit. Downie and his party soon found themselves in a very sticky situation. In January 1918 the revolutionaries in Finland, aided by Russian troops, gained control of Helsingfors and the southern half of the country. Communications with the north were cut; the British were without mail, without money, isolated in a country where brutal murders had become commonplace, and armed with only their personal weapons. The submarines were ice-bound in Helsingfors harbour. The Russian crew of the depot ship, where the British had their mess, turned hostile.

Fortunately the party had a large supply of navy clothing and tobacco, and by 'flogging' boots, coats, woollen underwear and tins of tobacco to the Finns enough money was obtained to buy provisions and other necessities. Then the British *chargé d'affaires* and his staff were withdrawn from St Petersburg and passed through Helsingfors on their way home, leaving Downie and his men more isolated than ever. Captain Cromie, however, was still at the Embassy, trying to cope with a chaotic situation in the same determined manner as when taking the *E-19* to do battle. He, too, arrived in Helsingfors – to give orders to Downie that the submarines were to be destroyed destroyed forthwith.

The Bolsheviks had accepted Germany's peace terms, and

under the Treaty of Brest-Litovsk all the British submarines in the Baltic were to be surrendered to the Germans. Cromie had obtained a reprieve from the Russians but there was no time to lose, for the Germans were advancing on St Petersburg to restore order and were about to send troops to Finland to aid the White Army there.

Downie had need of an ice-breaking tug in order to take the submarines out into deep water and blow them up, but he met with refusal when he asked the harbour-master for the services of a tug. Downie countered by regretting that he would therefore be obliged to destroy the submarines where they lay, and much damage could be caused to harbour installations – and (though he left this unsaid) to the tug-master's house, which was within fifty yards of where the submarines were berthed. Less than half-an-hour later the tug was breaking up the ice round the submarines; then it led a sad procession out of harbour. Downie was in command of the *E-1*, followed by the other three E-class boats in the charge of the Russian officers who had been on liaison duties with the flotilla.

The *E-1* and *E-19* were the first to be destroyed. They were secured alongside each other, the primers were inserted in the charges, and the alarm-clocks were set for an hour ahead – to allow for their inaccuracy. The scratch crews boarded the tug, which withdrew to a safe distance. Just before the hour was up there came a sheet of flame followed by a cloud of smoke from the two submarines, and when this cleared there was only an expanse of ruffled water where they had been. Meantime the *E-8* and *E-9* had been prepared for their end. The latter blew up and disappeared, but the former remained on the surface undamaged until well past the time for which the clocks had been set. Downie bravely boarded her – the tug-master was reluctant, understandably, to take him alongside, and needed a little persuading by Downie's revolver – and he found the flaw in the electrical circuit. The second attempt to blow up the *E-8* was also unsuccessful; she obviously knew this was no way to end her valiant career. The daylight was fading by then, so Downie decided to leave her there in the ice and destroy her with the C-class boats next morning.

On 5 April 1918 the British Submarine Flotilla in the Baltic ceased to exist, and the care and maintenance party was left with the problem of escaping and getting home. The Germans were less than twenty miles away. Fortunately there was a train leaving for St Petersburg, but competition for places on it was very strong. Downie and his men, carrying a minimum of kit, found the station seething with Russian soldiers and sailors who had been demobilised and were equally eager to get home. When the train entered the station the submariners rushed for a coach and held it with fixed bayonets against all comers. Captain Cromie arrived to see them off and shook hands with each man; he was staying on in Russia. (Three months later he was brutally murdered by the Reds in his office at the Embassy.)

Downie and his party had to wait several days in St Petersburg, staying at the Embassy, for a train to Murmansk, which was occupied by British forces. The Russian capital 'presented a picture of appalling desolation,' Downie wrote later in his report. 'Most of the shops had their windows smashed, and the few that remained open had little or nothing to sell. In nearly every street lay the rotting corpses of horses, which no one troubled to move, and everywhere one saw men, women and children of all classes on the verge of starvation.'

The British party left St Petersburg with members of the diplomatic corps and their families, and the eight-hundred-mile train journey to Murmansk took five days. At one point, just north of the Arctic Circle, the railway line had collapsed; after a long wait, all the passengers trudged half-a-mile to change to a filthy train which arrived from Murmansk for them.

A fortnight later the submariners were on their way back to England aboard a troop transport, marking the end of an epic in British submarine history.

4 A Case of Piracy, October 1927

In the summer of 1927 a gang of Chinese pirates was having a very successful season. They had no vessel of their own with which to attack and capture ships, but their method of operating eliminated the need of one – and made them more difficult to apprehend. The leaders had brought their method almost to perfection. They had a good intelligence service and planned ahead, sending some of their men to travel as ordinary passengers in a ship on a scheduled run which they had marked as their next victim; these men carried out a reconnaissance of the ship, noting any guard or security arrangements. On her next voyage, the gang would go aboard with other coolie passengers and, when at sea, at a given signal rush the bridge and seize the ship. Her officers were then forced at gun-point to take the ship to a notorious pirate haunt, Bias Bay, some thirty miles up the China coast from Hong Kong, and there the gang would loot the ship and rob the passengers and hold some of them for ransom.

It was all efficient and business-like – and often murderous. The Royal Navy on the China Station was asked to take more vigorous action against this and other pirate gangs, and for the first time in history a submarine was sent to check piracy on the high seas. A flotilla of old L-class submarines – they had come into service towards the end of the First World War – was based on Hong Kong, and one of these, *L-4*, was fitted with a small searchlight and then sailed to patrol off the entrance to Bias Bay. Her commander, Lieutenant Halahan, had orders to stop and search any ship attempting to enter the bay. Halahan had to keep his presence secret, so by day he remained submerged at periscope depth and at night patrolled on the surface without lights. The *L-4*'s crew of thirty-six officers and men spent an uneventful week in this manner, until the night of 20 October 1927.

Three nights previously the steamer *Irene* had sailed from Shanghai on her regular run to Hong Kong with deck passengers and general cargo. Her master was a Norwegian and three of his officers were British, but she belonged to the China Merchants Steam Navigation Company and flew the Chinese flag. Early on 19 October she put in at Amoy, her last port of call before Hong Kong, and there embarked more Chinese coolie passengers. Among them, had the master but known, were nearly a score of pirates with revolvers and automatics hidden in their bed-rolls. They were the 'executives'; the reconnaissance of the ship had been carried out on her previous voyage.

When the *Irene* was a few miles out from Amoy and the captain and most of his officers were at breakfast in the saloon, some of the pirates burst in brandishing their weapons. They had chosen their moment well, and the officers were at once overpowered. Others of the gang rushed the bridge, where the chief officer was on watch, and in a minute the ship was in the hands of the pirates. Some remained in the engine-room, threatening the engineers, while those on the bridge made the chief officer at the point of a pistol keep on course for Hong Kong, so that everything should appear normal on board to passing shipping. Their attention to detail was such that when a British warship was sighted they had the effrontery to dip the *Irene*'s ensign in salute! Meanwhile a dozen of them were systematically rifling the ship and robbing the passengers.

Late next day the *Irene* altered course for Bias Bay. As night fell the pirates darkened ship and stood in for the coast. They were entering the bay, believing that once again the operation had gone as planned, when a signal flashed out from low in the water calling on the *Irene* to stop. The master, who was on the bridge but under guard, rang down to the engine-room to comply with the order. One of the pirates at once threatened to shoot him unless he went full speed ahead. And pirates on deck were taking pot-shots at the vessel which was daring to challenge them.

Lieutenant Halahan switched on his searchlight, and when he had the *Irene* in its beams he ordered his gunnery officer to fire a blank warning round. This had no effect; in fact the *Irene* increased speed. The submarine chased after her and fired another blank round; the *Irene* still held on her course.

Halahan had definite orders to stop and search any suspect ship, and there was no doubt that this one had been hijacked. But her crew and passengers were very likely still on board, and if he opened fire in earnest there would almost certainly be casualties among innocent people. Yet what else could he do? He sent a live shell whistling across the bows of the *Irene*, and a great waterspout shot up ahead of her; but still she did not stop.

There was nothing for it. While Halahan held the *Irene* in his searchlight, the gun crew carefully aimed a shot at her hull, low down aft, thus hoping to cripple the ship and bring her to, without harming the passengers who were crowding the deck. The shell from the four-inch gun crashed into the engine-room and severed the pipes from the boilers; there was a great hiss of escaping steam, and the *Irene* lost way. The only casualty was one of the pirates who was about to shoot the chief engineer for not getting more speed out of the engines. But the shell also started a fire which soon spread.

Panic broke out. There were more than two hundred passengers on board the *Irene* – far more than the boats could hold. Many dived overboard, while the pirate gang seized two of the boats which the officers were trying to lower. Screams and shouts and revolver shots filled the night air as the *Irene* drifted helplessly with flames flickering from her stern.

Halahan took the *L-4* alongside the burning ship and began taking off passengers, a task made even more difficult and dangerous by the terror-stricken Chinese and the trigger-happy pirates. Some of the *L-4*'s crew kept diving into the sea to rescue those people who had jumped overboard to escape from the flames. The radio operator had already sent out calls for assistance; another submarine, a cruiser and a destroyer had all replied that they were making for the scene. Among the Chinese rescued from the water were several women and girls completely naked and hysterical. But the *L-4*'s crew were no less resourceful than the pirates. The First Lieutenant spotted some bales of silk floating away from the *Irene*; these were hauled aboard the submarine and each of the nude women was wound in a long length of silk, which served the double purpose of suppressing hysterics and keeping the proprieties.

By midnight the *Irene* was blazing from stem to stern, and Halahan stood off. He then had 222 survivors on board. All the *Irene*'s officers were among them, and probably a few pirates too. But it was no time or place to sort out the Chinese; with the *L-4*'s crew, there were 258 people in the 230-foot-long submarine. However, Halahan did take the precaution of ensuring that no Chinaman allowed below was carrying arms. Only four of the survivors were seriously injured; one was a cabin-boy who had been shot by the pirates, the other three were passengers who were badly burned.

Halahan cruised around to pick up any Chinese still in the water and to look for the pirates who had escaped in boats, probably with their loot. There was no sign of them, so he presumed they had got ashore, and he set course for Hong Kong. A naval tug had left there to tow in the *Irene*, but she burnt out and sank before she could be brought into harbour. Her owners were definitely not pleased with the Navy's intervention.

Halahan safely disembarked all his passengers at Hong Kong. He and his crew had at least taught the pirate gang a lesson; no more was heard of them, and piracy in the area became less frequent.

However, there was an unfortunate sequel for Halahan. In the spring of 1928 the *L-4* and others of her class were recalled from the China Station and sailed for England. There the veteran *L-4* was used to try out several life-saving devices, including a large pipe and valve to which a flexible tube could be attached outside by divers; the idea was to succour a sunken submarine by passing supplies down the tube. It was affectionatelyy called the 'bacon-and-egg tube', but never got beyond the experimental stage. Lieutenant Halahan missed seeing the *L-4* being used as a guinea-pig; he also missed his well-deserved leave in England. The owners of the *Irene* had sued him for damages of £53,000 for 'wrongful sinking' of their ship, and this had necessitated his remaining in Hong Kong. The China Merchants Steam Navigation Company probably thought the Admiralty could well afford such a sum and was unaware of the pressing need for economy in the Royal Navy at that time, for as an afterthought the Company put in a claim of £100 a day for loss of use of the ship. The case took fifteen months to reach the High Court in Hong Kong, so this claim attained considerable proportions.

It was all to no avail. The Company lost the case, for Halahan's counsel put in a plea that the sinking of the ship was 'an act of State'. Halahan was at last free to return to England, and he was then awarded the Distinguished Service Cross.

5 Submarine *Thetis* Missing! June 1939

The first of June 1939 was a warm, sunny day, and when shops and offices closed many people cycled or drove out into the country or to the seaside, complacently ignoring the war-clouds rolling up over Europe.

At a quarter-to-six that evening a telegraph-boy in Gosport had a puncture while on his way to deliver a wire to the duty officer at Fort Blockhouse, the Submarine Base. It had been received at 17.38, having been relayed via Liverpool and London from a tug at sea, and it cautiously asked 'What was the duration of *Thetis*'s dive?' The boy mended his puncture, cocked a leg over his red-painted bicycle, and finally handed in the wire at 18.15. An hour or so later the evening newspapers were carrying the headline 'Submarine *Thetis* Missing!' The public waited anxiously for more news, but none came that night. Next morning the eight o'clock BBC news opened with the sensational announcement that the stern of the *Thetis* had just been found poking out of the sea and that a destroyer was already standing by. People went off to work greatly cheered and looking forward to dramatic news of rescue during the day.

However, the men in the *Thetis* had already been submerged for eighteen hours, and intelligent rescue operations had hardly begun. Moreover, there were fifty passengers in the *Thetis* as well as her full crew of fifty-three officers and men, which meant that the toxic carbon dioxide was building up at almost double the normal rate. The Admiralty issued a statement that the submarine could remain submerged for at least thirty-six hours; but this applied only to one of her class diving with a normal complement. In any case, at the time little was known in the Submarine Service as to the real rate of deterioration of the air in a closed-down submarine. In point of fact, when the stern of the *Thetis* was at last located the one hundred and three men in her were already in desperate straits, many of them near to death. Meanwhile no one in high authority was taking vigorous, urgent action.

The *Thetis* had slipped away from Cammell Laird's shipyard at Birkenhead shortly before ten on the morning of 1 June to make her first sea-diving trials. She was 275 feet long and displaced 1,100 tons, had six torpedo-tubes, and her estimated maximum surface speed was sixteen knots. Two others of her class had already been completed, but the *Thetis* was the first to be built by Cammell Laird. The fifty passengers on board were chiefly yard technicians, civilian and naval observers, including Captain Oram, the senior officer of the flotilla to which the *Thetis* would be attached. This was the recognized routine when a new submarine went to sea before being officially accepted by the Navy. Despite the crowded conditions, there was a general feeling of relief at getting to sea at last after months of preparation and shipyard activity. The trials this day were to check the submarine's diving machinery and to adjust her underwater trim. The routine was well established; the thought that anything could go wrong never entered anyone's head. Cammell Laird was one of the two principal firms building submarines for the Royal Navy and had a high reputation for reliability and sound construction.

A civilian tug, the *Grebecock*, with a submarine liaison officer on board, joined the *Thetis* as she passed down the murky Mersey river. The tug's duty was merely to follow the submarine and to warn away any passing shipping during her trials. By 13.30 hours the *Thetis* was thirty-eight miles out of Liverpool and about fifteen miles north of the Welsh coast. The sea was calm, the weather clear and visibility excellent. Half-an-hour later the captain of the *Thetis*, Lieutenant-Commander Bolus, gave orders to take her down, having made a signal that he would be diving in the area for the next three hours. None of the passengers, not even the two caterers who had served the special cold lunch provided by Cammell Laird, had wished to be transferred to the *Grebecock* beforehand, though Bolus had twice asked them over the inter-com system.

The conning-tower was cleared; air hissed out of the top of the ballast-tanks and sea-water gurgled in from below, while the submarine moved slowly forward with her hydroplanes on ten degrees of dive. It was quite rightly a gentle and careful operation, but when all the ballast-tanks were flooded the *Thetis* was still on the surface. However, there was nothing alarming in a brand-new submarine's being unable to dive on her very first attempt. Bolus was merely annoyed that the underwater trim calculations had erred so much on the safety side. He gave the order to flood the auxiliary tanks, then increased speed. The *Thetis* went a little deeper, but half of the conning-tower was still above the water and there she remained. It was as if she knew.

Her captain ordered an inspection to make sure that all the water to weight her down was actually present. The calculations for her underwater trim drawn up by Admiralty officials from information supplied by Cammell Laird included the flooding of two of the six bow torpedo-tubes, numbers five and six, the bottom tubes of the two tiers. Each was supposed to have 800 pounds of water in it. The presence or absence of 1,600 pounds of ballast right up in the bows could easily make all the difference between diving or not diving. So the Torpedo Officer, young, curly-haired Lieutenant Woods, went forward to check the tubes. The *Thetis*, at this early stage of her trials, was not carrying any torpedoes.

Woods conscientiously checked all six tubes, beginning at the top with number one and two, by lifting the handle of the test cock fitted on the rear doors. The four upper tubes were empty, and he also inspected them for any signs of leakage from the sea by opening the rear doors and shining his torch up to the bow caps. All four were satisfactory. He then tried number six tube, as it was directly below number four. When he opened the test cock some water seeped out, indicating that the tube was at least half full. He moved across to number five on the starboard side, and nothing came out when he lifted the test-cock handle. (The tiny hole in this test cock was blocked by thick enamel paint, and this had been overlooked by the shipyard and naval inspectors.)

So Woods went on to inspect the interior of number five, calling to Leading Seaman Hambrook to come forward and open the rear door. Hambrook heaved on the lever; it was stiff, hard to move, whereas the others had swung over freely. Woods gave him a hand, and between them they pulled the lever over. With a crash, the rear door was torn from their hands and the sea cascaded into the compartment.

'Tell control-room, blow main ballast, we're flooding fast through number five tube!' Woods shouted to the men in the next compartment, the torpedo-stowage room.

He and Hambrook scrambled aft, the water rising round their legs and the submarine's bow already canting downwards. Helped by the men in the torpedo-stowage compartment, they struggled frantically to shut the watertight door. Unlike the other doors, it had no control lever to operate all the clips; each of these had to be fitted individually into its slot. And one slipped down and prevented the door from shutting tight. Meanwhile the sea-water was pouring through into the torpedo-stowage compartment.

Every man there knew that the submarine could be brought to the surface with one compartment flooded, but not with two. They also knew that just aft of the torpedo-stowage compartment, where the water was already up to their knees, was the mess compartment and under it the batteries. If the sea-water got into that compartment and down among the batteries it would react with sulphuric acid to form clouds of chlorine gas. And to choke to death on chlorine gas is a most unpleasant way to die.

Swiftly weighing things in the balance, Lieutenant Woods ordered a retreat to the mess compartment. The water-tight door between that and the still-filling torpedo-stowage compartment had a single control lever. In a moment, once everyone was through, the door was slammed shut and locked.

In the control-room, Lieutenant-Commander Bolus had ordered full speed astern while compressed air was roaring and hissing into the ballast tanks and forcing the water out of them. But the submarine which before would not go down, now would not go up. Despite everything that could be done, she pointed downwards more and more and, just as Woods and his men closed the door on the torpedo-stowage compartment, she hit the bottom at an angle of about forty degrees. The time was 15.00 hours.

Bolus and his Number One, Lieutenant Chapman, and Captain Oram went forward to assess the situation. While they were inspecting, the submarine's stern began to settle and half-an-hour later she was nearly level on the bottom, one hundred and sixty feet down.

A marker buoy was released, and the officers held a hurried

discussion in the wardroom. The official policy for escape from a sunken submarine was by use of individual DSEA sets (Davis Submerged Escape Apparatus, consisting of an oxygen bag worn on the chest and connected by a breathing tube to a mask with nose-clip and goggles; the inflated bag helped to keep the escaper afloat). But escape training in those days was carried out in tanks only fifteen feet deep. Moreover, instructions were that escapes should not be made until rescue vessels were known to be waiting to receive survivors on the surface. The diving area had been deliberately chosen well clear of the busy shipping lanes into the Mersey; the *Thetis* had no means of getting in touch with the *Grebecock*; and the submarine would not be reported 'missing' until she failed to surface at 17.00 hours, the end of her trials period. Furthermore, although there were enough spare DSEA sets on board for all the extra passengers, many of these men had never been trained in their use.

Bolus made the decision to try and surface the submarine. In theory, this was possible. A man wearing a DSEA set would enter the flooded torpedo-stowage compartment through the forward escape chamber, which had a door opening into it, make his way to the bows and close the rear door to number five tube; then open the drain valves and return the way he had come. The main ballast pumps would be started – fortunately the *Thetis* still had plenty of electric power in hand, thanks to Woods' snap decision – and the flooded compartments could be drained. Then the *Thetis* could surface normally.

In practice, a super-human effort was required. In that depth of water the man would have the breath half squeezed out of him by a pressure of over fifty pounds per square inch while he negotiated the two water-filled compartments, removing obstacles and doing what he had to do, and then made his way back. There was also the risk of being poisoned by breathing oxygen under pressure.

Bolus explained what was required and called for volunteers. Several men were willing and among them were two officers, Woods and Chapman. Their captain chose the latter as it was his job to know every detail of the submarine. He put on his DSEA set and entered the escape chamber. The time was 16.00 hours.

As the water rose about his body, so did the pressure. An iron band of pain tightened round his head and ears. Bolus and Oram, peering through the glass port, saw him make urgent signs to be let out. The chamber was drained down and Chapman stumbled out, weak and shaken, trembling with the cold and miserable at his failure.

Woods at once went to take his place; but in the meantime it had occurred to someone that if he succeeded in reaching the open torpedo tube but failed to return, the forward door of the escape chamber would remain open. It was therefore decided that two men would enter the escape chamber together, one to remain there to close the door if the other did not return. CPO Mitchell volunteered to accompany Woods. The two entered the chamber together but when it was half flooded Mitchell was seen to be in distress, and again the chamber was drained down to release him. Woods had felt capable of carrying on, and he offered to make another attempt with a fresh partner. PO Smithers, the second coxswain, volunteered. Woods put on another DSEA set and returned to the escape chamber with Smithers. This time it looked as if they would make it – at least, that Woods would be able to proceed forward. The watchers saw him grasp the clips of the door, but then Smithers began making similar frantic gestures as had the previous two men.

It was no good. And each time the escape chamber was flooded and drained, an hour of precious time was lost. The forward escape chamber, unlike the one aft, was not fitted with a drainage system; the water had to be got rid of by men forming a bucket chain to the bilges aft, a long and laborious process. By the time Woods and Smithers had recovered and got into dry clothes and the chamber had been emptied, it was 19.00 hours.

The *Thetis* was now two hours overdue in surfacing, but there were no indications that she was being searched for, let alone that her location had been found. The recognized signal to a sunken submarine that rescue was at hand was the dropping of a dozen underwater charges.

The situation was becoming desperate. The air was getting progressively worse; the carbon dioxide content was inducing a feeling of lethargy and making clear thinking difficult. There was no chemical absorbent such as soda lime carried in the *Thetis*.

While some energy remained, another attempt to escape by their own means was discussed in the wardroom and then put in hand. The submarine was too deep down, the pressure was too great for the escape chambers to be used; but if the stern could be raised again, by pumping out the after trim tanks and shifting water from aft to forward, there would be much less pressure over the after escape hatch. To do this would require some extra, makeshift piping, but some of the shipyard technicians declared they were capable of tackling the job. The little food remaining from lunch was shared out and passed around.

And so the men in the *Thetis* pumped and panted, worked and prayed, feeling the angle of the deck increase as the stern rose slowly towards the surface. . . .

Aboard the tug *Grebecock*, no one had liked the way in which the *Thetis* had suddenly disappeared; after trying for nearly an hour to submerge, she had quickly gone down amid an unusual foaming of water at her bows. And two hours later, when she had failed to carry out any of the manoeuvres previously arranged, the submarine liaison officer on the *Grebecock*, Lieutenant Coltart, became really worried. But the tug's radio was on the wrong frequency to have intercepted the *Thetis*'s diving signal, so he could not be sure that Lieutenant-Commander Bolus was keeping to the original schedule. It seemed impossible that a brand-new submarine could have met with any trouble in a calm sea only a few miles from land, and Coltart did not want to cause unnecessary alarm. He waited another half-hour or so, then decided to send a cautious signal to Fort Blockhouse. It had to be in clear, for he had no means of coding his message, and as the tug's radio-telephone could only just reach a radio station near Liverpool it would be transmitted from there via the GPO system. So Coltart worded his message in a non-committal way and hoped that it would prompt the Submarine Base into action.

This it did. When the telegraph-boy delivered the wire, an hour-and-a-half after Coltart had sent it, the staff at Fort Blockhouse had been anxiously phoning around for news of the *Thetis* and trying to contact her by radio. Now they ordered a search of the area where she had dived, and signals were made to various vessels to get under way at once. By then it was nearly 19.00 hours. Darkness would begin to fall in two and a half hours.

A flotilla of Tribal-class destroyers, whose maximum speed of thirty-six knots made them the fastest in the world, weighed anchor and put to sea – from Portland Harbour, some four hundred miles from the scene of disaster, and without a single experienced submarine officer on board. The mine-laying submarine *Narwhal* also sailed from Portland, but as the fast destroyers could not be expected to reach Liverpool Bay much before noon next day, the sending of the *Narwhal* was little more than a gesture. More to the point was the order to the deep-diving vessel *Tedworth*, which had some of the navy's expert divers on board, to proceed to the search area. But she was at Inveraray, over two hundred miles away; and, being a coal-burning ship, had to call in at the Clyde to bunker. Apparently no one in authority thought of collecting the divers and their gear and flying them to Liverpool, then transferring them to a fast destroyer or launch. The alert had been given, but the response – alas for the unfortunate men in the *Thetis* – was typical of the slack and haphazard manner in which the nation went to war three months later.

However, a destroyer, the *Brazen*, happened to be on passage from the Clyde to Plymouth and was only fifty-five miles from the search area when the alarm was raised. But she was steaming with only one boiler alight and took time to work up to maximum speed. The sun had almost set when she found the tug riding at anchor and was informed of the *Thetis*'s intended course underwater. A few minutes later, four Ansons came sweeping low over the area to make a hurried search before darkness set in. More than four hours had passed since Lieutenant Coltart had sent off his message and the *Thetis* had become officially overdue. The hours must have seemed very long to Coltart and the tug's crew, alone on an expanse of water where one hundred and three men were entrapped in the depths; and the first signs that a rescue operation of sorts was under way could not have made a very cheering impression.

The *Grebecock* was a harbour tug and had no means of checking her position at sea; she had continued sailing gently along when the *Thetis* finally disappeared from view, and had then drifted several miles before anchoring. Consequently she had not sighted the submarine's marker buoy; and the diving course which she gave to the *Brazen* sent the destroyer off in the wrong direction. To make matters worse, one of the

Ansons spotted a fisherman's buoy in the dying twilight and reported it as a submarine's marker buoy. The result of all this was that the *Brazen*, her searchlights sweeping the surface and her Asdic probing the depths, spent all night in wasted effort, scouring a wrong expanse of sea while the air in the *Thetis* continued to turn to poison.

But even if the *Brazen* had found the marker buoy it is difficult to see what could have been done in the way of rescue with the means at hand.

Sunrise was soon after five, and the *Brazen* – still alone in the area except for the faithful but inadequate *Grebecock* – extended her search with desperate tenacity. And soon after 07.30 hours her vigilant lookouts sighted the stern of the *Thetis* protruding from the water like an imploring finger. Lieutenant-Commander Mills, the *Brazen*'s captain, brought his ship swiftly but carefully close to the dark hull with part of the hydroplanes showing. Eighteen feet of it was angling up out of the sea, and nearby bobbed the marker buoy. The *Brazen*'s radio began sending the exact position of the *Thetis*, and her whaler pulled away to drop the twelve underwater charges which meant 'Rescue is at hand, escape at once.'

Mills hailed the *Grebecock* to come alongside, and Coltart went aboard the destroyer to advise about the next move. The Mersey salvage vessel *Vigilant* had come out from Liverpool during the night and could now be seen emerging through the haze. At this time, however, the *Tedworth* with her expert deep-sea divers still on board was in the Clyde and beginning to take on coal, having had to wait for the working day to start.

Suddenly there was a swirl of water alongside the pathetic protruding stern and two heads bobbed up. The whaler was still in the water and raced to pick up the two men; a few minutes later they were helped aboard the *Brazen* and given medical attention. The two were Captain Oram and Lieutenant

Woods, and taped to each man's wrist was a roll of oilsilk containing a message written on a sheet of signal pad:

From *Thetis*. On the bottom. Depth 140 feet, 16 degrees bow-down. Fore ends and torpedo-stowage compartments flooded. No. 5 bow cap and rear door open. Compartments evacuted. H.P. air required to charge submarine through either gun recuperator connection or whistle connection on bridge. Diver required to tighten down fore hatch so that blow can be put on forward compartments without lifting hatch. Strongback required on hatch as soon as possible. Keep constant watch for men escaping through the after escape chamber.

Oram and Woods were in bad shape but between them managed to tell their rescuers that conditions in the *Thetis* were desperate. They had already entered the escape chamber when they heard the underwater charges exploding. In fact Lieutenant-Commander Bolus had decided that the escapes should begin in any case, while some strength still remained, and had chosen Oram and Woods to be the first because their knowledge of the *Thetis* and of submarines in general would be of most value to the rescue operations. During the night, Bolus and his officers had worked out a plan to inject compressed air into the *Thetis* and force out the water in the forward compartments, and the details were put into the message carried by Oram and Woods.

The *Brazen*'s radio sent out urgent calls for the necessary equipment and specialists. The *Vigilant*'s one diver had no experience beyond depths of ninety feet; the air-hose aboard the salvage vessel was not long enough, and in any case she did not carry an air compressor.

Time passed all too quickly, while men stared down from the rail of their ship at the water around the stern of the *Thetis*, waiting anxiously for more heads to appear. Two boats were in the water, ready to haul any escaping men aboard. Their crews hammered in Morse on the exposed plates of the submarine, 'Come out, come out'. Again and again the message was pounded on the steel hull, but no reply came.

By ten o'clock the *Thetis* had been submerged for twenty hours. Suddenly bubbles appeared on the surface and first one and then another man appeared, tearing off his escape mask and gasping for breath.

The two were taken aboard the destroyer. They were Leading Stoker Walter Arnold, a tall, husky man, and Frank Shaw, short and stocky, a Cammell Laird engine fitter. When they had recovered a little they had a shocking story to tell. Most of the ninety-nine men in the submarine were unconscious if not dead; the others were too weak to scramble up the slope to the escape chamber. Lieutenant-Commander Bolus was propped against the engine-room door, but Lieutenant Chapman was still active; it was he who had been operating the controls of the escape chamber. Before their own escape, Chapman had sent four men into the chamber in a desperate attempt to increase the rate of escape, but they had been unable to open the hatch and were dead when recovered from the chamber. This had a most depressing effect, and Arnold thought that resignation set in then. He, however, was a powerful man and found a willing partner in an escape attempt. They, too, had difficulty in pushing up the hatch after the chamber was flooded.

As Arnold reached up and released the clip, Shaw put up one hand to push against the hatch. It did not move. Instinctively he kept pushing harder, then felt Arnold's hand on his arm. The water had to come a little higher to equalize the pressure, Arnold indicated. Then Shaw tried again, and the hatch moved. There was light – and life. Shaw felt himself shooting upward. For a brief moment before Arnold heaved himself up through the hatchway he let his mind expand. 'I'll make it now . . . even if the set packs in, I shall cope. Thank God.' He banged into a wire or two, then he broke surface and could feel the air on his face. 'Here you are, mate,' a voice called.

By the time Arnold and Shaw had finished telling their story, more vessels had arrived on the scene. The eight destroyers came slashing up from the south-west, still in perfect formation after their all-night dash; reducing speed, they fanned out and hove to. It was a brave sight but of no help to any men still alive in the *Thetis*.

A launch took the flotilla commander, Captain Nicholson, across to the *Brazen* and he assumed charge of operations. There was little he could do except bring himself up to date with the situation. No more salvage vessels had come out from the Mersey. The *Tedworth* had at last finished coaling and sailed, but she had nearly two hundred miles to go. However, Captain Nicholson ordered the *Vigilant* to loop a light wire round the stern of the *Thetis*, as there was no guarantee it would stay up of its own accord.

No more heads popped out of the quiet sea, though the men in the boats twice saw bubbles break the surface. Midday came and went, and with it the time when slack water would have enabled the deep-sea divers to operate best. Then the tide began pressing down on the submarine, and her stern sank lower in the water. The worried men in charge of operations thought of all kinds of desperate measures, but the only practicable one seemed to be to cut a hole in the stern – if some cutting gear were available. Failing that, an attempt was made to remove the small manhole cover of the *Thetis*'s after trimming tank which was just above water. It was highly improbable that any man could be dragged out that way, but some air might be pumped in; and any attempt was better than just standing by and waiting for experts and their equipment to arrive.

Mr Brock, the Wreck Master from the *Vigilant*, was rowed over to the stern, and he climbed on to the slippery metal armed with a screwdriver and a wrench. As he loosened the bolts of the manhole cover, fetid air hissed out. He was no submariner, and sent back for advice. He clung to his precarious perch while a debate went on aboard the *Vigilant*. He could hear no sound from inside the *Thetis*. Meanwhile the stern was beginning to twist and shift. Then back came a message to re-secure the manhole, in case it flooded, and to return to the *Vigilant*. A tug had arrived from Birkenhead with oxy-acetylene gear, and she and the *Vigilant* went alongside the stern to begin cutting a hole in it. The work had hardly got under way when the wire round the stern snapped loudly, the two ends flailed back across *Vigilant*'s deck — and the *Thetis* slid quietly beneath the surface. It was 15.10 hours on 2 June, and there were ninety-nine men dead in the stricken submarine.

Three hours later, salvage pontoons and lifting craft came surging across the bay from Liverpool and began energetically to try and bring the *Thetis* back to the surface. This work went on all through the night and the following day too, but the submarine remained stubbornly on the bottom. At 16.10 hours on 3 June, fifty hours after the *Thetis* had made her fatal dive, the Admiralty announced that all hope of saving those on board must be abandoned.

The nation was stunned by the tragic ending. It seemed incredible that those ninety-nine men could not have been rescued when for seven hours the position of their submarine was known and they were separated from their rescuers by only a few feet of water above the escape hatch. It seemed that much better efforts could have been made. An example of what was possible was given by four civilian divers who were working in Scapa Flow when news reached them of the desperate situation of the *Thetis*. They had already offered their services to the Admiralty five hours earlier and been courteously told it was not necessary; now came another message asking for their assistance. Their leader, Thomas McKenzie, called them up from the 140 feet of water in which they were working; they piled into a motor-launch and headed for shore, pulling off their diving-gear. At the nearest airport they found a small plane to fly them to Inverness – though they had to leave their diving-gear behind – and there transferred to a larger aircraft which flew them down to Liverpool. An urgent phone call had resulted in a destroyer waiting to take them out to the *Thetis* when, after a hair-raising drive from the airport, they reached the docks two hours after leaving Scapa Flow. But the message had been sent to them too late; soon after it reached them in Scapa Flow, the *Thetis* had slipped to the bottom. When they got down to her, having borrowed some diving-gear from the assembled salvage vessels, their signals on the hull met with a depressing silence.

A Public Inquiry was opened in July. The Admiralty set up its own committee under Martin Dunbar-Nasmith, V.C., DSO (then Admiral Sir) to make recommendations to avoid a repetition of the disaster. The findings of the Inquiry were not very conclusive, and the war prevented the committee's recommendations from being implemented; they were chiefly that escape training with DSEA sets should be carried out in tanks at least thirty feet deep.

The major factor that emerged was the urgent need to have located the *Thetis* before nightfall on the first day. The build-up of carbon dioxide was greater than anyone had thought possible – including Bolus and his officers – and the official statement that all the men had died from carbon dioxide poisoning in less than forty-eight hours was received at the time with amazement and disbelief. Bolus's decision to raise the stern and the consequent activity for much of the night had increased the rate of pollution of the atmosphere; but if everyone had sat around doing nothing but conserving oxygen, not even four men would have been able to escape from the depth of water in which the submarine was lying.

The real culprit, however, was never known: whoever blocked the hole in the test cock with thick enamel paint or whoever left the bow cap open after flooding number five tube.

All but two of the crew of the *Thetis* had died, but the submarine herself was resurrected. She was raised to the surface and taken back to Birkenhead in November 1939. The war on land was quiet, but at sea the navy was finding plenty of opportunities of engaging the enemy, and submarines were badly needed. By November 1940 the *Thetis* was at sea again, re-named *Thunderbolt*. The only reminder of her tragic past was a rusty high-water mark which ran slanting along the sides of some of her compartments, and which no amount of paint could conceal for long. Her new commander, Lieutenant C.B.Crouch, had told the men joining her: 'There is going to be no fuss about this boat just because she was once called *Thetis*. Each man who joins will be allowed the opportunity of declining to stay. After that he will be expected to get on with it. And there will be no backward glances.'

But such is the spirit in the Submarine Service that no man declined to stay.

Thunderbolt's first war patrol was off the Gironde estuary, on the west coast of Occupied France. On the morning of 15 December she sank an Italian submarine with a stern-on hit — a spectacular shot at any time, but in a first-ever attack it was without precedent.

Some six months later, after an uneventful stint of escorting convoys halfway across the Atlantic from Halifax, the *Thunderbolt* was posted to Gibraltar. While on passage, Crouch received a signal to try to pick up the survivors from a British freighter, the *Guelma*, which had been torpedoed midway between Madeira and the Canaries. Early next morning the submarine reached the position which the freighter had radioed at the time of her sinking. Crouch surfaced, found the boats and took the shipwrecked crew on board. They numbered forty-three, including two stowaways; and Crouch had a crew of fifty-nine. It was an amazing and awesome coincidence — just two years after the *Thetis* tragedy, the submarine's compartments were again crowded with one hundred and three men.

Crouch set course for Gibraltar, and for two days kept on the surface the whole time. Then, one day out from his destination, he decided to dive to check the trim. Nothing unexpected occurred. This time the submarine carried the one hundred and three men out of danger to safety.

From August 1941 to February 1942 the *Thunderbolt* operated in the Mediterranean, still with Lieutenant-Commander Crouch, DSO, as captain. She took part in some 'cloak-and-dagger' activities off Crete and Greece, but added little to her bag as shown on her 'Jolly Roger' until the fifth patrol. Then, in the space of three weeks, her crew torpedoed an escorted merchantman, sunk a U-boat and an armed trawler by gun action — and were attacked at various times by five destroyers and an Italian seaplane, and were on the receiving end of more than sixty depth-charges.

Thunderbolt returned to Britain for a long refit, then she was posted to the Mediterranean again. There were many new faces among the crew, but Crouch was still in command. In March 1943 they were on patrol off the west coast of Sicily, and one dark night attacked an Italian convoy escorted by a sloop. Crouch manoeuvred to fire a single torpedo at a large steamer, registered a hit, then dived deep to twist and turn away from the depth-charges of the avenging escort vessel. Desperately *Thunderbolt* tried to escape, but the Italian was even more tenacious; the captain was a former submariner and well able to meet Crouch's tactics. The deadly cat-and-mouse game continued for twenty-four hours, until the submarine was fatally shattered by a pattern of depth-charges. And once again she showed the tip of her stern before sinking to the deep bottom of the Mediterranean.

6 A Great U-Boat Captain, 1940–March 1941

Another depth-charge. Water hit the U-boat's still side with the sound of tinkling glass. The crew could hear the searching destroyer grinding and threshing several fathoms above – and wondered if they could be heard too, or rather that bloody fool who had just dropped a spanner. There's another! Stay still as statues. Sometimes, so it's been said, a U-boat can be heard groaning like a whale. The air was foul and dank, for the boat had been submerged a long, long time. Would it ever end? Think of something else, of green fields, the girl back home, of anything but submarines and a slow panting struggle for life. Steady there! A terrific punch on the hull; then another; and another. This is it then. The men at the hydrophones were sitting rigid, tense. And the captain, how was he feeling? Kapitänleutnant Otto Kretschmer, the man whose job it was to get them out of this. 'Silent Otto', the enigmatic, the martinet, but not a bad bastard after all.

This was the *U-99*'s first patrol, and almost her last too. For twenty-two hours she was bombed and depth-charged, but eventually escaped with a twisted periscope and leaking oiltanks. She was able to make Bergen, then Wilhelmshaven, where she went into dock for repairs. Kretschmer and his crew of forty-three had nevertheless sunk 62,000 tons of Allied shipping in ten days.

When the *U-99* next put to sea, in late July 1940, Otto Kretschmer had orders to operate in the grey, tumultuous waters of the North Atlantic. He was then twenty-eight and had been a submarine commander for three years, a highly professional and experienced officer who was dedicated to the task of depriving the enemy of as many ships as possible. He spoke English well and knew the West Country, having studied for a time at Exeter University before the war. He had quiet confidence in himself as a seaman and a fighter, all quite justified, and he commanded his U-boat with an iron hand, yet succeeded in winning the respect and loyalty of his crew. He had none of the exuberance and conceit of many of the other successful U-boat commanders; nor was he, like his First Lieutenant, von Knebel-Döberitz, an arrogant Nazi. A man of few words, he was difficult to know; hence his nickname of 'Silent Otto'.

The summer of 1940 was a grim time for Britain. Having lost the land battle in Flanders, the British seemed likely to lose the sea battle too – the Battle of the Atlantic, of convoys and their inadequate escorts against the increasing number of U-boats able to use the French Atlantic ports, and their new 'wolf-pack' tactics. The British were losing ships twice as fast as others were being built. It was a fight to the death, of unrestricted warfare now; gone were the days of stopping ships and examining papers. But this did not mean that every restraint was cast aside; the pitiless rule of war is to kill and destroy the enemy, but both in U-boats and British destroyers there were human feelings for survivors, for the men in a lifeboat or on a raft. British and German commanders alike fought with everything they had, but they did not fight the defeated survivors. Although to surface and assist a shipwrecked crew in their boats was an unjustifiable risk for a submarine, Kretschmer had done just that on several occasions, giving in English the course and distance to the nearest land; and on one occasion a bottle of spirits was handed down to warm the insides of a boatload of soaked seamen.

The *U-99* was one of the V11/B type, an ocean-going submarine of 750 tons armed with twelve torpedoes, one four-inch gun and two ack-ack guns. In Kretschmer's hands, and with a fine crew, the submarine became a formidable weapon, a killer of ships, and made her commander's name a legend in sea warfare.

On 28 July the *U-99* was off the south-west of Ireland and sank the 13,000-ton *Auckland Star*. Two more freighters were torpedoed and sunk before the end of the month. Then, north of Ireland, Kretschmer sighted a west-bound convoy escorted only by an old destroyer, the *Daring*, and a corvette. The convoy was pursuing a zizag course at a speed of eight knots. Kretschmer gained an attacking position, torpedoed the destroyer and then the 6,000-ton *Jersey City*. The *U-99* was depth-charged by the corvette for more than an hour, but escaped unhurt. That night Kretschmer returned to the convoy and torpedoed three more freighters, but they were only damaged and succeeded in making port. Kretschmer tried to sink the third ship by surfacing and shelling her; he found himself opposed by a very determined skipper who returned his fire so effectively that he gave up the chase. With all torpedoes expended, Kretschmer made for Lorient, where his flotilla was now based.

This was a new experience for the crew of the *U-99*. They had sailed from Germany . . . and now the lookouts on the bridge sighted a blue-grey line on the horizon – the coast of France. They gazed eagerly towards it as the U-boat steered between Breton fishing-boats with brightly-coloured sails. A German mine-sweeper hove in sight and signalled 'Welcome to France'. As the *U-99* edged into harbour the men mustered on her deck could see Germans in uniform waving to them. Kretschmer, wearing his best brass-bound cap, tossed away the butt of the black cigar he had been smoking and glanced at the golden horseshoe fixed to the side of the conning-tower. There was one on the other side too; they were a pair which had been found strangely entangled in the *U-99*'s anchor when she had first got under way at Kiel back in April. Once again they had brought him luck, and this time a hero's welcome; he was awarded the Knight's Cross for his total of 117,000 tons of enemy shipping sunk.

Kretschmer soon took the *U-99* to sea again and during another short patrol sank seven ships totalling 56,000 tons. The usual tactics of a U-boat attacking a convoy was to fire three or four torpedoes fan-wise from one of the flanks, on the assumption that if they missed the ships in the outer column they were more or less bound to hit two or three in the inner columns of the convoy. Kretschmer had different ideas, which were expressed with Germanic precision in his Standing Orders:

U-99 will abide by my principle that fans of torpedoes fired from long range are not guaranteed to succeed and must prove wasteful. It should not be necessary to fire in the first instance more than one torpedo for one ship.

The principle stated above makes it necessary that we should fire at close range, and this can be done only by penetrating the escort's anti-submarine screen and at times getting inside the convoy lanes. This should be the objective of all our attacks.

These highly individual tactics were one reason for his success. The convoy's escort of destroyers and corvettes would be dashing up and down the flanks of the columns to search for the attacking submarine.

Nor did Kretschmer believe in diving after firing torpedoes and making off at an angle to the torpedo tracks, to escape from the depth-charges of avenging destroyers, as did other submarine commanders, British as well as

German. His Standing Orders numbers ten and eleven read:

Once an attack has been opened we must not, under any but most desperate of circumstances, submerge. As a general rule I alone must decide when to dive. This instruction is based on my belief that a submarine on the surface can manoeuvre at high speed to avoid danger, and if necessary can fight back with her speed and fire power in torpedoes. If we are being chased, it is a general principle that once a submarine submerges and loses the use of speed she is at the mercy of the hunter.

Remember that at night on the surface it is almost certain that you will see a surface vessel far sooner than she will see you. This applies to enemy destroyers and other anti-submarine vessels which might detect you with their Asdics the moment you dive, but would be unaware of your presence if you ran away on the surface.

The character of the man was revealed in other parts of his Standing Orders:

Lone ships, not flying neutral flags or carrying a Red Cross sign, and in every other way giving the appearance of behaving as a belligerent, should be sunk by gunfire if possible to conserve torpedoes for more difficult escorted targets. They may be torpedoed if gunfire is obviously impracticable.

Survivors are to be assisted if there is time and by doing so the submarine is not exposed to undue danger. The crew should realize that if *U-99* be sinking and there is time to abandon ship they would expect to be rescued by the enemy. That is precisely what the enemy have a right to expect from us.

In normal circumstances *U-99* will use daylight hours for shadowing a convoy and working up to a favourable attacking position by nightfall. A favourable attacking position is on the dark side of a convoy when there is moonlight, so that the convoy will be silhouetted to us, while our small bows-on silhouette will be almost impossible to detect.

When there is little or no moon, *U-99* will always attack from the windward side of the convoy. Enemy lookouts peering into a wind and sometimes rain and spray are less efficient than those with their backs to the wind.

The realism of Kretschmer's bold tactics was abundantly proved in October when the *U-99* joined with six other U-boats in attacks on convoy SC7, an action which has become known in the Battle of the Atlantic as 'the Night of the Long Knives'. It was one of the earliest wolf-pack actions of the war. On the afternoon of 16 October Kretschmer's radio operator picked up a sighting report from a U-boat which had found a big, eastward-bound convoy. Kretschmer changed course and increased speed to intercept. Two days later he sighted the slow-moving thirty-four ships of the convoy and its four escorts, and all afternoon he cruised just below the horizon some fifteen miles south of the convoy, conforming with his Standing Order number five: 'Only attack convoys by day if it is not convenient to wait for darkness . . .' Among the other U-boats closing in on the convoy were two whose captains had, like Kretschmer, already sunk nearly 200,000 tons of Allied shipping. One was Günther Prien, the brilliant and conceited 'Bull of Scapa Flow', commanding the *U-47*; the other was the flamboyant Joachim Schepke, commanding the *U-100*.

It was a dark and rainy night as the seven U-boats began to close the convoy, not in a pre-arranged or coordinated attack (they were of course observing radio silence) but each with the aim of sinking as many of those thirty-four ships with their vital cargoes as possible. Kretschmer headed for the starboard flank of the convoy; one ship had already been hit and was on fire. The *U-99* slid into the convoy's columns between two zig-zagging destroyers a mile apart, her low silhouette practically invisible in the dark and the rain-squalls. Then Kretschmer set to work. He hit a freighter dead amidships, missed another then heard the third torpedo boom against the hull of a ship in the next column; she broke in two and went down in less than a minute. Everywhere, like a pack of wolves, the U-boats were at the convoy. Ten thousand tons of petrol went up in a fiery ball a thousand feet high; an ammunition ship exploded with a deafening roar. Some ships stood on end before disappearing, others listed heavily and tried to limp along.

The escorts were racing up and down the flanks of the convoy, which had made a starboard turn, firing a barrage of starshells to find the submarines outside their screen which were sending torpedoes into the formation of ships. There were certainly U-boats out there, and they were making hits, but there was another inside the formation itself and doing more deadly damage, making nearly every torpedo count. Down in the bow compartment of the *U-99* men were toiling and sweating to get the spare torpedoes into the tubes. The bunks on either side had been lashed up out of the way; the torpedoes were manhandled into position and with many a heartfelt wish disappeared from sight.

When Kretschmer had only two torpedoes left he decided that he had played his luck hard enough for one night, and he slowed to let the convoy – what was left of it – pass ahead. Then he saw a straggler and could not resist firing the two torpedoes he was keeping for self-defence. The first missed but the second hit, and the freighter began to settle low in the water. Another U-boat surfaced on her opposite side from the *U-99* and sank her with gunfire.

It was then two in the morning of 19 October; Kretschmer ordered a course for Lorient and went below for a nap. Twenty of the thirty-four ships in the convoy had been sunk, seven of them by the *U-99*. When she returned to base Kretschmer was welcomed and congratulated in person by the U-boat C-in-C, Karl Dönitz.

On his next patrol, the *U-99*'s fifth, Kretschmer sank three ships, two of them being armed merchant-cruisers. This brought his total of shipping destroyed to well over 250,000 tons, and he and his crew were well and truly fêted when they returned to Lorient. The crew were sent to a luxury rest-camp; Kretschmer was called to Berlin to be decorated by Hitler himself with the Oak Leaves to his Knight's Cross, the highest decoration then possible, and he was given the State box at the Opera for a performance of *Tannhauser*. None of this was much to Kretschmer's liking; he greatly preferred dining with his friendly rivals Prien and Schepke at some country res-taurant in Brittany, and supervising the refit to his submarine. He and the other two U-boat aces, who had each sunk about a quarter-of-a-million tons of shipping, made an agreement that the first to reach 300,000 tons would be wined and dined by the other two. Dönitz tried by all means short of a direct order to get Kretschmer to accept a training command ashore, for his experience and enthusiasm would be invaluable to the new U-boat officers; but Kretschmer by every respectful means refused.

He took the *U-99* out on patrol again on 22 February 1941, with a military band on a small steamer playing him out of Lorient to the strains of *The Kretschmer March*, specially com-posed by the bandmaster in his honour. Prien and Schepke had sailed two days before to harry the convoy routes two hundred miles south of Iceland. The Atlantic was at its miser-able worst, with huge menacing seas and dark, rain-filled clouds sweeping low and reducing visibility. The *U-99* ploughed and bucked her way to where Prien in the *U-47* had reported he was attacking a west-bound convoy. Then a signal from Prien was picked up: 'Depth-charged. Contact lost. Am continuing pursuit. 22,000 tons sunk so far.' Two days later he reported another convoy, steering north-west. Kretschmer was close enough then to join in the attack after nightfall, but was forced to dive by destroyers. Once again the *U-99*'s crew stood motionless as they heard the enemy overhead and felt their submarine rock and shudder as depth-charges exploded. But their luck still held; it was another U-boat destroyed that sent the British escort vessels away satisfied. Later in the day the *U-99* surfaced very cautiously and reported to base; in return Kretschmer was told to look for and finish off a ship that had been torpedoed during the night but was still afloat. She was the *Terje Viken*, a huge Norwegian whale-factory ship. While on the way to the position given, the *U-99*'s radio operator heard the base repeatedly calling Prien: '*U-47*, report your position.' But no answer came. Soon after dark on 8 March the *U-47* had been sighted on the surface by the destroyer *Wolverine*; contrary to Kretschmer's tactics, Prien had dived, been located by the *Wolverine*'s asdic, and was blown to pieces by a pattern of depth-charges. One of the three aces would never mark up 300,000 tons sunk.

Kretschmer searched in vain for the *Terje Viken*; he saw only a few boats carrying survivors and a destroyer hovering in the neighbourhood, which forced him to go deep.

A couple of days later he intercepted a signal from the *U-110* reporting a convoy eastward-bound off Iceland. This was the HX112, consisting of nearly fifty merchant-ships carrying supplies and munitions to a lonely beleaguered Britain. They were escorted by five destroyers and two corvettes commanded by the very experienced and redoubtable Commander Donald Macintyre in the *Walker*. He and his group had made rendezvous with the convoy in mid-Atlantic early on 15 March after successfully escorting a west-bound convoy to within six hundred miles of Halifax.

Schepke in his *U-100* was the first to reach HX112. Shortly before midnight on 15 March he crept to within a mile of the escort screen and fired four torpedoes fan-wise at the columns of ships. A 10,000-ton tanker carrying petrol burst into blinding flame. The *Walker* and other destroyers searched desperately for the U-boat responsible, zigzagging over a wide area, but without success. Next day the *U-99* arrived, and was sighted on the surface by the destroyer *Scimitar* when six miles distant. Kretschmer dived quickly and dropped back to wait for nightfall before attacking, in accordance with his Standing Orders. Meanwhile the whole convoy had altered course in an evasive manoeuvre, leaving him well astern.

By dark, however, Kretschmer had found the convoy again and slipped through the escort screen. Between ten o'clock and midnight he beat all his previous records by torpedoing and sinking five merchant-ships. The last two hits were obtained by firing simultaneously at two ships, each torpedo being set to turn ninety degrees, one to port and the other to starboard. They hit almost at the same moment; one ship sank, the other limped on, so Kretschmer fired two more torpedoes at the latter to be sure of her.

The destroyers were weaving about at high speed searching in vain for the almost invisible enemy. Their one hope was to sight a U-boat's tell-tale white wake on the dark and heaving waters, give chase to force her to dive, and so give the asdics a chance to bring the depth-charges into action. Commander Macintyre, on the bridge of the *Walker*, did sight a thin line of white water that could only be the wake of a U-boat. He increased speed to thirty knots and altered course towards the target. A swirl of phosphorescent water still lingered as the destroyer passed over the spot and sent a pattern of ten depth-charges crashing down. Great water-spouts rose to masthead height astern of the *Walker*, but no wreckage or other evidence of a kill appeared on the surface. The *Vanoc*, which was equipped with one of the early, primitive radar sets, came racing past to join in the hunt, and the two destroyers sent down pattern after pattern of depth-charges.

But while the escort vessels were actively chasing U-boats on the flanks of the convoy, the *U-99* was still in its midst. Kretschmer, however, had only one torpedo left and that was in a stern tube. He was sighted on the surface between the convoy columns by the tanker *J.B.White*, and her master turned and gallantly tried to ram the U-boat. Just then the tanker was struck by Kretschmer's last torpedo and brought to a standstill. With no sting left, Kretschmer began to withdraw from the action; he handed over to his officer of the watch and went below for a rest. It had been a long patrol, the *U-99* had been at sea for more than three weeks, and her captain was tired and weary; the long strain of operational command was beginning to tell at last.

While Kretschmer was looking forward to a quiet passage home, his colleague Schepke was wondering if the *U-100* would ever get there. His had been the U-boat attacked with depth-charges by the *Vanoc* and *Walker*, and the propeller shafts were so damaged that he was unable to stay submerged for long. He limped away, then surfaced to try to make sufficient repairs to get him home.

The moment the *U-100*'s conning-tower broke through the sea, a 'blip' appeared on the *Vanoc's* radar set. The destroyer increased speed and charged down the radar bearing. Schepke, in the conning-tower, saw the destroyer's bows come racing out of the dark at thirty knots. 'Don't panic!' he called to his men on the foredeck. 'He'll miss us astern!' Schepke was probably deceived by the *Vanoc's* camouflage painting, for a few seconds later he died horribly, crushed between the destroyer's bows and his own periscope standards. He too would not be there to pay for Kretschmer's celebration dinner.

'Have rammed and sunk U-boat,' *Vanoc* signalled to *Walker*. While the *Vanoc* was picking up the few survivors from the *U-100*, the *Walker* circled her protectively. Suddenly Macintyre's asdic operator excitedly reported 'Contact, contact!' It seemed incredible that there should be another U-boat in the area where one had just gone to the bottom. But Macintyre was not a man to miss a chance to kill a U-boat. When in doubt, attack. But the *Walker* had used up all the depth-charges in the throwers. Hurriedly the depth-charge party hoisted some more of the 300-pound 'ashcans' up from the magazine. The asdic contact strengthened as the *Walker* ran in to attack. A pattern of six depth-charges, all that could be got ready in time, was hurled into the water. As they exploded, the destroyer ran on to get sea-room to turn for further attacks; and then came a signal from the *Vanoc*: 'U-boat surfaced astern of me.'

It was the *U-99*. And she had come up between the two destroyers, her depth-gauge broken, the forward compartment flooding through a split pipe, and both main motors out of commission.

The *U-99* had been steaming fully surfaced and had passed near the scene of action between the *Vanoc* and the *U-100* less than half-an-hour after the U-boat had sunk. The young officer on watch had suddenly seen the *Vanoc* or the *Walker* about a quarter-mile on his starboard bow. Instinctively – and forgetting his captain's Standing Orders – he had ordered a crash dive and plunged down the hatch behind the lookouts. And the disaster that Kretschmer had foreseen, and tried to assure against, in his Standing Order number eleven had come to pass.

His submarine badly hurt and sinking towards depths where her hull would be crushed, Kretschmer had no choice but to blow his ballast. Even that was difficult, for the control lever was jammed and the combined efforts of two of the strongest members of the crew were needed to shift it. The *U-99* broke surface in a rush and fell back leaning heavily to starboard in a spreading pool of oil. Without torpedoes, helpless to fight back, Kretschmer told his radio-operator to send his last message: 'Destroyer depth-charged. 50,000 GRT. Prisoner of war. U-Kretschmer.'

Vanoc's searchlight stabbed the night and illuminated the U-boat. The guns' crews in both destroyers sprang into action, and, with more savage intent than accuracy, peppered the sea around the enemy's hull. Macintyre had picked up the crew of the *J.B. White* and they, avid for revenge, gave enthusiastic help to the ammunition supply parties, so that soon the *Walker*'s deck around the guns was piled high with shells. Then, amid the flash and whine, a signal lamp blinked across the spattered waters: 'From captain to captain. Please pick up my men drifting toward you. I am sinking.'

Kretschmer had given orders to abandon ship and to scuttle her. He stayed on deck, seeing that all his men jumped overboard, while Engineer Officer Schroeder went below to open the valves. As the *U-99* lurched and slid beneath the waves her crew swam in a kind of ragged formation towards the net hanging over the *Walker*'s side. Macintyre manoeuvred his ship to windward of the swimming Germans, and as he drifted down to them some of the British crew helped them aboard. A few were in the last stages of exhaustion from the icy cold of those northern waters. Three of the *U-99*'s crew of forty-four were missing – two had succumbed in the water and the engineer had gone down with the submarine.

Kretschmer was the last to clamber up the net, still wearing his brass-bound cap; and when he reached the *Walker*'s deck he found to his surprise that he still had his Zeiss binoculars slung round his neck. They were a very special pair presented to him by Admiral Dönitz, and he had always sworn that no enemy would ever get them nor board his submarine. He had made sure of the latter and now he tried to send his prized binoculars to the bottom. But one of Macintyre's officers was too quick for him; and Kretschmer's binoculars became very special war loot for

Macintyre, who used them for the rest of the war.

When the identity of the U-boat commander became known there was much satisfaction aboard the *Walker* at having disposed of Germany's crack submarine. Kretschmer had that night topped the 300,000-ton mark, but neither he nor his two fellow-aces would be having a celebration dinner in Brittany.

Next morning Kretschmer was walking on deck accompanied by Chief Engineer Osborne when he suddenly stopped in amazement, staring at the ship's crest, a horseshoe.

'What a coincidence! My submarine sailed under the sign of the horseshoe too, though it was the other way up from yours.'

'Yes, captain, we'd noticed that,' said the Chief. 'You had your horseshoe with the points downwards, the wrong way round. The luck was bound to run out.'

Kretschmer gave a rueful laugh. He had learnt that the *U-99* had not been sighted on the surface just before his junior officer had crash-dived. If his Standing Orders had been kept to, the *U-99* might well have escaped.

The convoy suffered no more attacks and safely reached home waters. Accommodation aboard the *Walker* was somewhat cramped, as she was carrying the master and thirty-seven crew of the *J.B.White* as well as the captain and forty-one crew of the *U-99*. There was no possibility in the small ship of keeping the prisoners segregated, and the merchant navy men had some digs at the Germans. But a *modus vivendi* was soon reached – only the arrogant von Knebel-Döberitz had to be put firmly in his place – and before the *Walker* docked at Liverpool her Chief Engineer, who was very keen on contract bridge, had got together a four consisting of himself, Kretschmer, the master and chief officer of the *J.B.White!*

Kretschmer spent the rest of the war as a prisoner in England and Canada. After the war he served in the Federal German Navy and until quite recently was a Captain on the active list.

7 Sunk by one of their own Ships, July 1941

On a day in July 1941 a convoy of merchantships escorted by armed trawlers and gunboats was moving steadily up the East coast, having assembled in the Thames estuary that morning. Included in the convoy was a brand-new U-class submarine, the *Umpire*, Lieutenant-Commander Mervyn Wingfield. She had been built in Chatham dockyard and was a comparatively small boat, barely two hundred feet long and displacing little more than six hundred tons, designed for operations close inshore off enemy bases. Her eventual destination was the Mediterranean theatre of war, but now she was bound north-about for the Clyde to carry out sea trials and training with the Third Flotilla. She had no escort duty with the convoy; on the contrary, she was under the protection of the escort.

Towards the end of the day a lone German bomber came in low from seaward and began attacking the leading ships of the convoy. The *Umpire*'s officer-of-the-watch, Lieutenant Edward Young, RNVR, gave the order to dive. The klaxon sounded and the submarine made her first-ever dive at sea and under way. All went well, but while the *Umpire* was submerged the convoy was drawing ahead; so a few minutes later, the enemy bomber having flown off without causing any damage, the *Umpire* surfaced and regained her station in the convoy.

As darkness fell the convoy was off the Norfolk coast and

began sailing through E-boat alley – so called because it was within reach of the fast German torpedo boats based in the captured Dutch ports. A number of treacherous sandbanks lie a few miles off this coast, and the strong currents have drawn many a vessel on to them. It is a dangerous stretch of water in peacetime, doubly so in wartime. Convoys could show no lights, each ship followed the one in front through the night, along the narrow swept channel, and if one vessel veered off course it was more than likely that several would do so.

But this time it was neither E-boats, mines nor sandbanks that brought disaster to the *Umpire*.

An hour or so after nightfall her port diesel engine developed trouble and had to be stopped while the engine-room staff under the Chief Engine-Room Artificer, G. S. Killan, tried to repair it. These attempts were unsuccessful and the submarine had to reduce speed. The captain flashed a signal to the Commodore of the convoy that he would have to fall astern, and a gunboat was detailed to drop back and escort *Umpire*.

Lieutenant Godden, the *Umpire*'s navigator officer, was on the bridge with two lookouts. It was a calm night but very dark. After a time, the gunboat lost touch with the submarine, and soon she was alone on the water and almost invisible to other ships. A south-bound convoy was known to be sailing down the same buoyed channel and was due to pass by the north-bound convoy at about midnight. Eventually the *Umpire*'s lookouts sighted the oncoming convoy, and Godden sent down a message for the captain to come to the bridge some of the ships were on the starboard bow. The normal 'rule of the road' is for ships meeting in a channel-way to pass port to port, in other words to keep to the right. Wingfield decided to ease away gradually to port, hoping that the oncoming ships would pass down his starboard side; at the same time he had to be careful not to stray from the narrow confines of the swept channel.

The first six ships of the convoy, contrary to the Regulations for Preventing Collision at Sea, did pass down *Umpire*'s starboard side at a distance of about two hundred yards, probably without sighting the submarine low in the water. Then out of the darkness loomed an armed trawler, dangerously close. It was, however, her right of way, and according to the rules Wingfield should have altered course to starboard. But there was a continuous line of ships only two hundred yards to starboard. Wingfield ordered 'Hard a-port!' At that moment the trawler must have seen the submarine low and dark in the water, and turned instinctively to starboard. Collision was inevitable. Wingfield gave an urgent yell down the voice-pipe, 'Full astern together!' But the trawler had already struck the submarine hard on her starboard bow, tearing a gash in her pressure hull. She lurched to port, and for a few seconds the two vessels stayed locked together. Wingfield just had time to shout furiously, 'You bloody bastard, you've sunk a British submarine!' Then he and Godden and the two lookouts were swept into the sea as the stricken *Umpire* plunged to the depths.

The other two officers, Lieutenant Edward Young and the First Lieutenant, Peter Bannister, were in the wardroom. They jumped to their feet in alarm, and Bannister shouted the order, 'Shut watertight doors!' Most of the lights went out, and men came running and stumbling aft from the crew compartments forward as the bow of the submarine dipped downwards. 'Shut that bloody door!' Bannister yelled to Young, who was holding the door to the wardroom open, unable to bring himself to deny a chance to anyone still alive while water was not actually coming through. The watertight door further forward must have been slammed shut by the impact – or deliberately closed by someone at the sacrifice of his own life. The truth was never known, but many of the crew were given the chance to get aft and try to escape.

Young clamped shut the door he was holding, though with some difficulty because of the angle of the boat, and struggled aft to join the others in the dark control-room. By now, *Umpire* had sunk to the bottom. Surprisingly, no water was coming down the conning-tower hatch; that, too, must have fallen shut under the shock of collision or when the boat took on a list. But water was pouring in from what seemed a hundred places, and the bewildered, stunned men were already knee-deep in it. The First Lieutenant called for lights, and some of the men began searching for the emergency torches, but without much success. The *Umpire*, like every submarine, was fitted with a number of them, but they were enclosed in sealed tin canisters painted dark grey; and in the blackness of a submarine without lighting they could not be seen. (In later submarines, these canisters had bands of phosphorescent paint put round them.)

Young remembered that he had a torch in his drawer in the wardroom, and he sloshed back to find it. As he returned with it to the control-room he shone it on the depth-gauges and was surprised to see them resting on the sixty-foot mark. This meant that the *Umpire* was in shallow water, so he suggested to Bannister that it might be worth trying to blow her up, despite the weight of water in her forward compartments. Bannister agreed and opened up the valves until all the ballast tanks were blowing, but the depth-gauges did not budge.

The water was climbing relentlessly higher, and there was the fatal danger of chlorine gas if the sea-water reached the battery cells under the deck. (The water was in fact coming in through the ventilation shaft which had been fractured by the impact, but no one had thought of shutting the bulkhead ventilation valve, which would have stopped the flow of water. The problem of escape would still have remained, but would not have been so desperately urgent.)

Lieutenant Edward Young gave a vivid description of the situation in his book, *One of our Submarines*, which he wrote after the war and is probably the best book ever written about wartime service in operational submarines:

In the half-darkness the men had become anonymous groping figures, desperately coming and going. There was no panic, but most of us, I think, were suffering from a sort of mental concussion. I discovered one man trying to force open the watertight door that I had shut earlier. 'My pal's in there,' he was moaning, 'my pal's in there.' 'It's no good,' I told him. 'She's filled right up for'ard and there's no one left alive on the other side of that door.' He turned away, sobbing a little.

For some reason we decided it would be useful if we could find more torches. I knew there must be one or two others somewhere in the wardroom, so I made yet another expedition down the slope, wading through the pool that was now waist-deep and already covering the lowest tiers of drawers under our bunks. I spent some time in the wardroom, shivering with fear and cold, ransacking every drawer and cupboard, pushing aside the forsaken paraphernalia of personal belongings – underclothes, razors, pipes, photographs of wives and girl-friends. But I could find only one torch that was still dry and working. Holding it clear of the water, I returned to the control-room.

It was deserted.

The door into the engine-room was shut. Had I spent longer in the wardroom than I thought? Perhaps they had all escaped from the engine-room hatch, without realizing that I had been left behind. Even if they had not yet left the submarine, they might already have started flooding the compartment in preparation for an escape, and if the flooding had gone beyond a certain point it would be impossible to get that door open again. I listened, but could hear nothing beyond the monotonous, pitiless sound of pouring water. In this terrible moment I must have come very near to panic.

I could at least try hammering on the engine-room door. Looking round for a heavy instrument, I found a valve spanner and began moving aft towards the door. As I did so I heard a voice quite close to me say, 'Christ, who's that?' I looked up and found I was standing under the conning-tower. In it, to my infinite relief, I saw Peter (Bannister) with an able seaman and one of the ERAs. 'Where the hell have you come from?' said Peter. 'Where the hell's everybody gone?' I retorted. 'Any room for me up there?'

'We ought to be able to squeeze you in. The others are going to escape from the engine-room.'

None of the four had any escape equipment, but with the depth-gauges showing sixty feet the upper hatch of the conning-tower could not be more than forty-five feet below the surface. Bannister warned the others that there was a danger of hitting their heads on the bar joining the periscope standards as they went up; but the submarine's list to starboard should minimize the risk. First, they had to raise the pressure inside the tower. Bannister, at the top of the ladder, had already tried to open the hatch, but although he exerted all his strength it remained firmly shut.

Young, standing at the foot of the tower, opened the lower lid a little and air came hissing up – then, with it, came the dreaded stench of chlorine gas. Young stamped the lid shut again, and Bannister had another try at opening the hatch.

This time [Young wrote later] he managed without much effort to lift the hatch slightly off its seat, allowing a trickle of water to come through.

'Okay,' said Peter. 'Well, boys, take your time. There's

no hurry. You say when you feel you're ready.'

I said I was for having a go at once, before we weakened ourselves any further by breathing foul air, and the others agreed. We stripped down to vest, pants and socks.

'Ready?' asked Peter.

'Ready,' we all replied, though I think the ERA had reached the point in his sickness where he wanted to die more than anything else.

'Right, stand by,' said Peter cheerfully. 'Here we go for fourteen days' survivor's leave. We're off!' And he pushed up the lid with all his strength.

I took as deep a breath as I could, and then the sea crashed in on us. There was a roaring in my ears, a blackness everywhere, and there was nothing for it but to fight for life with all one's primitive instincts of survival. Hauling myself up by the rungs of the ladder, I found my head obstructed by the A.B's bottom. With the strength of a desperate man I pushed up at him, his heel struck me in the face, I pushed again, and then we were through the hatch and clear of the submarine. I swam upwards with quick, jerky breast-strokes. It seemed a terrible distance. Time stretched out of its normal span until I thought my lungs must surely crack before I reached the surface. And then suddenly I was there, coughing, spluttering, gasping in great draughts of the sweet night air and drinking in the blessed sight of the stars shining in the immensity of space.

The sea was fairly calm, with no more than a gentle popple. Seeing two heads in the water not far away, I called out and found they were Peter and the A.B., both in good heart. Of the ERA there was no sign. We could make out the dark shapes of several ships around us, so we began shouting to attract attention.

Meanwhile, in the engine-room, Chief ERA Killan had

started organizing the escapes through the hatch. There were seventeen men in the engine-room, one of them a civilian from Chatham dockyard. But only fourteen DSEA sets could be found in the engine-room lockers. Leading Seaman Band volunteered to go back into the control-room and look for more sets. The bulkhead door dividing it from the engine-room had already been shut (as Young had found), and Killan warned Band that if the water-level in there was found to be rising rapidly after the door was re-opened for him to go through, it might have to be slammed shut on him. Band accepted the risk, the door was opened and he went through. He fumbled around in the dark for a few minutes, then returned empty-handed, saying he had been unable to break open the DSEA lockers because the wires sealing them were too thick. (This was another matter that was corrected by the Submarine Escape Training organization, headed by Captain W.O.Shelford, and a quick-release catch designed by him was later fitted on all DSEA lockers.)

Three men volunteered to go out through the escape hatch without a DSEA set, and each sought out his closest shipmate and arranged to cling to that man's legs on the way up to the surface. The civilian was fitted with a set and its simple operation was explained to him by PO Shorrocks. Then Killan detailed another Petty Officer, Bill Treble, to go through the escape drill with each man before he left the submarine. It seemed comparatively comfortable in the engine-room; there was warmth from the starboard engine, which had been running until the moment of sinking, and the bulkhead door shut out the ominous sound of rushing water and the choking smell of chlorine. No one felt there was any urgency – or perhaps the mounting carbon dioxide in the crowded engine-room was already bringing on a feeling of lassitude. . . .

The senior ratings roused themselves to action. Killan ordered the flood valves to be opened, and as the water and the pressure rose he asked for a volunteer to go up and open the hatch. Everyone had clambered on top of the engines, which were still giving some warmth; as the submarine was lying in comparatively shallow water, the engine-room had to be flooded for only about two-thirds of its height in order to equalize the pressure to that of the sea outside. Again it was Band who took the risk. *Umpire* was equipped with a 'Twill-trunk', a hoop-like casing normally raised concertina-wise and fixed to the escape hatch. This had already been extended and lashed down to special eye-plates on the deck, with a ladder hooked into it. The water now rose inside it. Band put on his breathing apparatus, ducked under the water and disappeared up the ladder. He was soon back to report that the hatch was open.

The flooding of the engine-room had brought up black oil from the bilges; the two men with torches shone them around and their light reflected a most uninviting spectacle. There was no sound of ships overhead, so the men had no idea what to expect when they reached the surface. Killan sent the men without escape sets and their companions up first, a couple at a time, and then the civilian. At intervals of five or six minutes a man moved across to the ladder, was quickly briefed by PO Treble, ducked under the greasy water and disappeared. When more than half the men had gone, Killan climbed into the Twill-trunk to make sure that the hatch was still open and that none of the escapers had got caught up in any obstruction. He had remembered the disastrous attempts to escape from the *Thetis*. But the way was still clear; instead of escaping there and then he returned to the engine-room, covered in black oil, and carried on supervising the escapes of the remaining men.

The senior ratings were the last to leave the submarine, an hour and more after the first couple of men had gone up. Lieutenant Young, who had been picked up by a gunboat, left the bunk where he was recovering from delayed shock and went on deck when told that more men were escaping from the *Umpire*. 'They were coming up at fairly frequent intervals, strange Martian creatures with their DSEA goggles and oxygen-bags, and rendered almost unrecognizable by black oil . . . but they were in extraordinary good spirits, half intoxicated with their unexpected return to life. . . .'

Three of the seventeen who escaped from the engine-room failed to make the return to life. The civilian, who had got into something of a panic, never reached the surface; and two of the three ratings without DSEA sets were unable to stay afloat long enough to be rescued. The buoyancy of the oxygen-bag might have made all the difference to the survival of these brave volunteers.

All the rescued men were taken to Yarmouth by various craft, and only then did Young learn that two of his fellow officers were missing. He and the able seaman were the only survivors from the group of four who had escaped through the conning-tower. Lieutenant Bannister had swum with the A.B. for a time and then disappeared, probably drawn under by the strong currents. Lieutenant-Commander Wingfield and the three men swept overboard had kept together in the water at first, but in the darkness and confusion the trawler's boat was a long time finding them. They were all wearing heavy clothing, and Lieutenant Godden had long seaboots on; the two lookouts were the first to go under, then Godden gasped that he was sinking. Wingfield supported him for a time; then he, too, sank from sight. Wingfield was unconscious when the trawler's boat reached him and hauled him from the water. He revived, and for a few hours had the terrible thought that he, the captain, was probably the sole survivor from the sunken *Umpire*.

In fact more than half the submarine's complement had been saved, making the highest percentage of survivors from any sunken British submarine. But it would have been a very different story if the depth of water where the *Umpire* went down had been forty or fifty feet more – or if the forward watertight door had not been slammed shut.

The good work performed by Chief ERA Killan was recognized by the award of the British Empire Medal. Lieutenant-Commander Wingfield was not held to blame for the collision; he was soon given another command, and during his distinguished wartime service in submarines won a DSO and two DSCs. Edward Young, too, had a very gallant career in submarines and ended the war as Lieutenant-Commander, DSO, DSC and Bar.

8 Six Men against a Fleet, December 1941

A great bluff was being carried out in Alexandria harbour in late December 1941. To all appearances, to the Italian reconnaissance aircraft which daily flew over the port, Admiral Cunningham's flagship, the *Queen Elizabeth*, was a sea-going warship. She was on an even keel with her waterline showing; the routine was as usual, with the ceremony of 'Colours' every morning and the admiral himself on deck saluting the Ensign and the Royal Marines' band playing. But in fact the ship was sitting on the bottom of the harbour with a hole forty feet square in her hull. The true waterline was twelve feet below the surface; the visible one had been painted on by dozens of men during the night.

Another battleship in the harbour, the *Valiant*, had been so badly damaged that she had to be put into dock; and a destroyer, the *Jervis*, was temporarily out of action. All this was the work of three Italian midget submarines crewed by six intrepid men. If Admiral Cunningham had but known at the time, the fleet at Alexandria had been saved from greater damage by a disastrous setback to the Italian exponents of midget submarines more than a year earlier.

The Italian Navy was the first to develop these 'human torpedoes'. Even before Italy entered the war in June 1940 a research team had begun work in a country house near the naval base of Spezia. In close collaboration with the First Submarine Flotilla, this team produced a midget submarine intended to be carried near to its objective by a large submarine and which could be armed with torpedoes or mines. This was followed by the *Maiale* – literally 'pig' – or SLC (*Siluro a lenta corsa*, slow-running torpedo), which could be compared to a midget submarine as a motor-cycle to a mini-car. It was in fact a manned underwater-charge, a torpedo-like craft with two seats and a detachable warhead containing a delayed detonator. An electric motor drove the *Maiale* at a speed of only two or three knots. The crew of two rode astride wearing protective suits and breathing apparatus. Though they generally carried out their approach to the target with just their heads showing above water, the crew were otherwise fully submerged for several hours.

In August 1940 the Italian Naval Command mounted an attack on the British fleet at Alexandria, then full of capital warships. Four *Maiali* and their crews were sent aboard a sloop, the *Calypso,* to the deserted bay of Bomba in Cyrenaica, some three hundred miles west of Alexandria, where they were to rendezvous with the carrier submarine *Iride* and a depot ship. At Bomba they were to transfer to the *Iride,* which would take them to the vicinity of Alexandria.

All went well at first. By the morning of 21 August the little flotilla was gathered in the shallow waters of Bomba bay. The 'pigs' had been transferred to the *Iride* but their crews were still on board the *Calypso,* which was moored alongside the depot ship to refuel; the submarine was preparing to put to sea to make a check dive to adjust her trim. Suddenly, just before noon, three Swordfish from the carrier *Eagle* came roaring in low over the sandhills surrounding the bay. The centre aircraft made straight for the *Iride,* while the other two flew down either side spraying her deck with their machine-guns.

The submarine commander could do no more than point his vessel at the centre Swordfish to present as small a target as possible, while his anti-aircraft guns blazed defiance; the water was not deep enough to make an emergency dive, even if there had been time to do so. A torpedo dropped from the plane's under-carriage into the sea and a moment later struck the *Iride* forward of the conning-tower. There was a shattering explosion, the submarine reared half out of the water and then plunged to the bottom of the bay. Her commander and others on deck who had survived the machine-gunning just managed to jump clear before she sank. But nine of the crew went down in her, imprisoned in the after torpedo compartment.

The three Swordfish roared away, mission accomplished – though their flight-lieutenant and his admiral's staff were unaware of the true purpose of this small concentration of enemy vessels.

The depot ship had been hit too and was sinking. But the *Calypso* had received little damage; she slipped her moorings and hurried to the aid of the submarine's crew. The *Maiale* men, all expert divers, plunged over the side and found the *Iride* lying in less than thirty feet of water. Though badly damaged forward, she seemed intact aft; one of the swimmers, Lieutenant Luigi Durand de la Penne, was sure he heard shouts for help from the after compartment.

Back on board the *Calypso* a hurried council was held. The only way of effecting a rescue was to open the after escape-hatch from the outside. Lieutenant Durand de la Penne and his colleagues put on special diving-masks and went down again and again. By tapping on the submarine's hull they were able to communicate with the imprisoned men, but they found the hatch had been distorted by the explosion and all their efforts failed to shift it. They kept trying until far into the night, even risking further air attack by burning powerful underwater lights.

Early next morning a steel cable was let down to the submarine and shackled to the obstinate hatch. The winch on the ship's deck slowly turned until there was a violent rattle and the cable went slack. The *Maiale* men dived down and found the hatch open – and two dead petty-officers in the flooded compartment. They must have been drowned while trying to force the hatch. There was no sign of the remaining seven men.

The divers put on masks and went down again. By tapping on the hull and shouting through their masks which were fitted with speech diaphragms they discovered that the seven men were still alive in a compartment further aft. But the bulkhead door which they had shut behind them could be opened only from their side. The rescuers could do nothing to help them until they helped themselves.

It was fully realized that as the men had been entombed for about twenty hours the air they were breathing must be very foul and consequently they were not only weak but lethargic, without the will to make an effort to save themselves. Something had to be attempted, nevertheless. The divers swam down and shouted to the trapped men: 'Open the door from your side. Hold on against the rush of water, and when an air-lock forms dip down and swim out, and we'll be waiting for you.'

There was no response. The seven men were confined in a small space; by now they would be suffering from headaches and nausea, and unconsciousness and death would soon follow. They had to be spurred by some means into taking immediate action.

The divers went down and signalled on the hull: 'If you do not open the door in the next thirty minutes, we shall abandon you.' They returned to the surface hoping that the absence of activity around the submarine would rouse the men to attempt their last chance of escape before it was too late.

110

The minutes sped past and nothing happened. Nearly everyone on board the *Calypso* was staring over the side, waiting tensely to see a swirl of water which would tell them that the men were coming up. When the half-hour had almost passed the surface was broken by a cloud of bubbles and a man appeared in the midst of it, arms flung upwards and shrieking with relief. In a moment the *Maiale* crews were diving down to the submarine and helping more men to the surface. Durand de la Penne even swum into the shattered hull and through the opened bulkhead, where he found two of the men still hesitating; he hauled them out, and other divers came to his assistance. All seven survivors were got aboard the *Calypso,* but two died later from the effects of their long entombment.

This setback to the Italians' plans did not deter them for long. In October the submarine *Scire,* Lieutenant-Commander Prince Valerio Borghese, successfully carried some *Maiali* to the western end of the Mediterranean and their crews penetrated Gibraltar harbour; but the attempt ended disastrously for the *Maiale* men, though they only just failed to score a hit on the battleship *Barham.* The Italians did not give up trying, and on a third attempt to attack shipping at Gibraltar, nearly a year later, the *Maiali* succeeded in sinking two vessels. Encouraged by this, another operation was mounted against the shipping in Alexandria harbour, where the only two British capital ships remaining in the Mediterranean were moored.

Three teams were briefed to take part. The leaders were Lieutenant Durand de la Penne, now a veteran 'human torpedo' (he had participated in one of the attempts at Gibraltar and only just escaped being made prisoner), Captain Antonio Marceglia and Captain Vincenzo Martellotta, all naval officers. The submarine *Scire,* still commanded by Lt-Commander Borghese, was again to be used to carry the *Maiali* to the harbour approaches. The operation was planned with great care. Italian bombers were to attack the harbour as the *Scire* approached, in the hope of creating a diversion. The submarine would then send off the three *Maiali*, and when these reached their objectives the detachable warhead of each would be fixed to the keel with the aid of special clips; afterwards, the crews were to scatter small incendiary bombs about the waters of the harbour, the idea being that these would set fire to the fuel-oil escaping from the damaged ships. Another submarine, the *Topazio,* would lie off the Rosetta mouth of the Nile that night, and the following night, to pick up any survivors of this hazardous operation who managed to get out to her.

The attack was due to go in on the night of 17 December, but rough weather caused Lt-Commander Borghese to put it back twenty-four hours. When his submarine surfaced at 18.40 hours the following evening, about 2,500 yards north of the mole light, the weather was perfect for the attempt – a moonless night with a calm sea and clear sky. The three *Maiali* were launched and set off on their mission, while the *Scire* made her way back to Leros.

The six 'human torpedoes', wearing their breathing apparatus and with only their heads above water, reached the harbour entrance at a lucky moment – just as the boom had been opened for some destroyers returning from patrol. Durand de la Penne skirted the French squadron moored in the harbour (this was Admiral Godfroy's force which had been demilitarized after the French armistice in 1940), and soon after 02.00 hours reached the battleship *Valiant.* He then discovered that his co-pilot, Bianchi, had disappeared and that his *Maiale* was sinking under him. He dived, caught hold of the torpedo and, working in blinding mud on the bed of the enemy harbour, dragged the warhead to about ten feet below the keel of the battleship and halfway along its length. He switched on the delayed detonator and swam to the surface, exhausted by his efforts. He discarded his breathing apparatus, and the fresh air revived him; he was about to swim towards land when there came shouts from the *Valiant* and the sounds of men running along her decks. Searchlights swept the water, and then came a few bursts of machine-gun fire. Durand de la Penne scrambled on to the *Valiant*'s mooring, where to his surprise he found Bianchi installed.

A few minutes later the two were discovered by a patrolling motor-launch, taken ashore and immediately interrogated. They produced their military identity papers, but quite properly refused to answer any further questions. Admiral Cunningham, who had been roused at four in the morning and informed of the incident, gave orders for the two to be taken aboard the *Valiant* and clamped in the bowels of the ship. If something serious were about to happen to the *Valiant* they might give the information in order to save their lives.

But they remained silent – until ten minutes to six. The explosion was set to take place at six. Durand de la Penne asked to be taken to the captain, and told him it would be advisable to abandon ship as she was due to blow up in a few minutes.

'Where are the charges placed?' Captain Morgan asked him.

The Italian officer refused to answer, and was taken below again. In the darkness he tried to cheer up Bianchi, but received no reply – for the very good reason that the other had succeeded in escaping from this dangerous situation. After a few more agonizing minutes, there came the expected explosion.

Durand de la Penne was lucky enough to escape hurt, and a little later found himself on the after-deck where Captain Morgan was giving orders to the fire-fighting teams. A few cable-lengths away could be seen the *Queen Elizabeth*, with a number of the crew massed in the bows. Then she, too, was shaken by an explosion and was distinctly seen to rise in the air. (Admiral Cunningham maintained that she rose five feet!) Debris and fuel were shooting out of her funnel.

This was the work of Captain Marceglia and his co-pilot, Schergat. Their attack had gone through almost exactly as planned. They had detached the warhead and suspended it about three feet below the *Queen Elizabeth's* keel by means of a length of cable. The two men had then surfaced and got astride their 'sea-pig' and made for land. After sinking their craft, by setting the special mechanism, they hid for a while among some rocks. Eventually they reached Alexandria and took a train out to Rosetta. But then their luck deserted them, and they never succeeded in getting out to the *Topazio*. Egyptian police captured them as they were going down to the beach.

The third team, Martellotta and Marino, had been almost run down by one of the destroyers while approaching their target, the carrier *Formidable*. Then they discovered that the aircraft-carrier was not at her moorings. (She had in fact been badly damaged during the evacuations from Crete seven months earlier.)

So instead they fixed their warhead to the hull of a large tanker alongside the destroyer *Jervis*. The tanker blew up and the *Jervis* was put out of service for a month. The two Italians got as far as the dock gates before being captured.

At 06.20 the duty officer on one of the unarmed French ships, the *Duquesne*, wrote in the log-book: 'Explosion similar to previous two on *Queen Elizabeth's* port bow and right under her. *Valiant* has a list to port and appears to be sinking by the bows. *Queen Elizabeth* listing to starboard.'

The cost to the Italians of putting two enemy battleships out of action was six specialists made prisoner.

The British Mediterranean fleet was left with only four light cruisers, while the Italians had five battleships and three heavy cruisers ready for sea. Fortunately for the outcome of the war, the Italians did not dare to take the offensive, but concentrated their efforts upon the approaches to Malta and protecting the supply convoys to Rommel in North Africa. But where individual action was concerned, the Italian Navy had shown itself as good as any.

After the Italian armistice there was an interesting sequel to the attack on Alexandria harbour. De la Penne was released from a prisoner-of-war camp and went to fight with the British underwater forces. In March 1945 he was being presented with the Italian equivalent of the V.C., the *Medaglio d'Oro,* for his attack on the *Valiant,* and Captain Morgan (then Vice-Admiral Sir Charles) happened to be present. Stepping forward, he took the gold medal and pinned it on the breast of the man who had knocked out his own ship three years before.

9 *Upholder*, the Killer of Submarines, 1941–April 1942

'All ready for sea, sir.' The First Lieutenant saluted his commanding officer as he climbed the steel rungs of the conning-tower.

'Thank you, Number One.' The CO returned the salute and that ended the official formality. 'Let go for'ard. Let go aft. Slow ahead, port...'

Lieutenant-Commander malcolm David Wanklyn was taking his submarine *Upholder* and her crew of three officers and twenty-eight ratings out from Malta on yet another patrol, the seventeenth in nine months.

In 1941 patrols in the Mediterranean tended to be short, because targets were frequent and torpedoes were quickly expended. Patrols also tended to be frequent, for submarines were in short supply. So were torpedoes, like much else in Malta, the besieged island; every one had to show a dividend. Ships in ballast were low down the list of targets. Primary objectives were warships and deeply laden troopships and transports taking reinforcements or supplies to Rommel in North Africa.

When the *Upholder* moved off from Lazaretto Creek and cleared the harbour boom this 7 November 1941, the success bars of her Jolly Roger already showed more than 100,000 tons of enemy shipping sunk and two cruisers badly damaged,

116

plus one 'cloak-and-dagger' landing on the coast of Sicily. Her crew had already gained eleven decorations, including the DSO and VC to the bearded, piratical-looking captain. David Wanklyn was thirty years of age and had been in the Royal Navy for sixteen of them. Despite his height of six feet two, in 1933 he had elected to serve in submarines, and since then had spent nearly half the time in the Mediterranean. He had met his wife in Malta and they were married there in May 1938, spending their honeymoon at the lovely Sicilian resort of Taormina. In August 1940 he was appointed to submarine *Upholder*, then merely a job number in a Barrow shipyard, and saw her grow into a sleek, lethal vessel a little under two hundred feet in length and displacing 630 tons. A comparatively small submarine with a maximum depth of only two hundred feet, she was designed for operating in coastal waters – in the event, those of the Mediterranean, for where she sailed in December. That was all right by David Wanklyn; they were almost home waters to him, and a battleground where the *Upholder* and her crew were badly needed.

Their successes in nine months of offensive operations had already made them a legend in Mediterranean Command; but more important was the fact that Wanklyn's daring, skill and qualities of leadership had earned him the respect and admiration of his crew – 'Good old Wanks!' they would say when he was out of hearing. His Victoria Cross, the first awarded to a submariner in the Second World War, had been won in May when the *Upholder* had sunk a strongly escorted Italian troopship, the 18,000-ton *Conte Rosso*, carrying thousands of reinforcements for the Afrika Korps. At the time the *Upholder* had only two torpedoes left and her asdic had been put out of action by depth-charge attacks earlier in the patrol. The *Conte Rosso*'s destroyer escort had come surging in for revenge, and only Wanklyn's coolness and superb handling of the submarine deprived of hearing aids had got her away unscathed.

Now this seventeenth patrol promised to be as fructuous. A Maryland aircraft had sighted an Italian convoy and escort east of Cape Spartivento, and a small squadron consisting of two cruisers and two destroyers sailed from Malta to intercept. This squadron was the famous Force K which for some reason always seemed to go to sea on Saturdays, and sure enough the alert had come on a Saturday, 8 November. The *Upholder* had been on patrol for less than twenty-four hours when she received a signal that Force K would be passing through her area during the night. And shortly before midnight Wanklyn and his crew heard the ships passing overhead – and smiled grimly to themselves. Would Force K still have been speeding to intercept if the *Upholder* had not sunk an Italian submarine in the vicinity a few hours earlier?

The British were not alone in having sighted an enemy surface force, for the Italian submarine had obviously been informed of the course that Force K was taking. She and the *Upholder* had both been on the surface, but the keen eyes of Petty Officer John Swainston, DSM, had sighted the other first in the dim light. Wanklyn had promptly dived to periscope depth and when within 1,500 yards of the still unsuspecting enemy had fired four torpedoes – a submarine kill was worth half the number he carried. One, if not two, had hit, and the stricken submarine had rolled and twisted and then disappeared beneath the waves. Wanklyn had surfaced and cruised around the oil-fouled waters, but no survivors had appeared.

When Force K had passed overhead, Wanklyn followed after; the surface ships were going to look for trouble, and that was where the *Upholder* wanted to be. Soon after one in the morning Wanklyn and the lookouts on the bridge had a memorable sight. The two cruisers, *Aurora* and *Penelope*, had driven off the Italian destroyers with their six-inch guns and were shooting up the transports and supply ships. Five vessels were blazing furiously, a large tanker was a wall of flame, and as the men on *Upholder*'s bridge watched they saw an ammunition ship give a superb display of fireworks before she blew up with a tremendous explosion. A great pall of smoke was drifting up to the velvety night sky.

Force K withdrew, its task completed. The *Upholder* remained. Wanklyn reasoned that after this catastrophic destruction some worthwhile targets would come hurrying to the scene. And when he put up his periscope at dawn there were three Italian destroyers hovering around the still-burning transports. One was even stopped, probably picking up survivors, and was right in his sights.

'Fire one.' The *Upholder* shivered slightly and lifted a little as the weight streaked from her bow.

It was a hit. But the sky now seemed filled with enemy aircraft, and Wanklyn went deep for a time. When he next poked up his periscope for a quick look round he saw the damaged destroyer down by the bows and being slowly towed away by her consort – and, obligingly drawing nearer, two enemy cruisers with a screen of four destroyers. This was a submariner's dream come true, but with one flaw – the *Upholder* was short of torpedoes. The four destroyers were zigzagging like drunken seamen, two on either beam of the cruisers, making a fanning probe of the waters. Wanklyn nevertheless skilfully manoeuvred for an attack on the nearest cruiser.

'Fire one, fire two, fire three.' The lot.

The first torpedo narrowly missed the cruiser but was not entirely wasted; it blew in the bows of a destroyer on the far side. The second torpedo went crazy, tearing around in circles instead of heading for the target; the *Upholder* was within its circling track and there was danger of being hit by her own torpedo, but then it streaked away and disappeared. The third skimmed past the cruiser's stern but hit the damaged destroyer, which was stopped; this second blow made her rear up and she slid beneath the waves in a matter of minutes.

Wanklyn rubbed his large competent hands together – the only sign he ever gave of his satisfaction – then, all torpedoes expended, he took evasive action and headed away from the area as fast as possible. But he still had a duty to perform; despite the risk he surfaced and made a signal to Malta giving the position and course of the two Italian cruisers. Others, either in the air or at sea, might be able to finish what he had begun.

On the way back to base some of the *Upholder*'s crew sewed three more bars on her Jolly Roger, and it fluttered triumphantly in the breeze as she entered harbour. She had been out on patrol for only eighty-seven hours, but how successful they were!

No military band played the *Upholder* into harbour; no grateful C-in-C presented Wanklyn with a fine pair of binoculars. There was no luxurious rest-camp on Malta, no restaurants serving gastronomic, black-market meals. Officers and men got what the rest of the island got – short rations. Even beer was in short supply. But what the fighting men missed most was their mail from home. So many mailbags went down with ships lost in convoys to Malta. Britain was being heavily bombed night after night, that much was known. But was home a smoking heap of rubble . . . did no letters mean . . .? The first thing the *Upholder*'s crew looked for on return to base was mail, and lack of it was damaging to morale. They did not even know whether their own letters were arriving.

It was New Year's Eve and the *Upholder* was about to go out on another patrol. The hard-bitten crew went below to their stations, some wearing overalls, others off-white long sweaters. Last aboard was the captain, his uniform jacket a little more shabby, his cap oil- and grease-stained, but his beard neatly trimmed.

'All ready for sea, sir,' reported newly-joined Lieutenant G.P.Norman.

'Thank you, Number One.'

Once again the *Upholder* slipped through the boom defence and picked up her local escort which would guide her through the swept channels. The familiar yellowish rock of Malta dropped astern. Trim dive completed in a few minutes, the submarine surfaced again and proceeded on her lawful occasions at a steady twelve knots.

'She's all yours,' Wanklyn said to the officer of the watch, and slipped below to the familiar smells. He placed his night-glasses where he could grab them in a moment and opened his sealed orders. This time his billet was off the west coast of Sicily, in waters where the Carthaginian war-galleys had barred the way to the west during the Punic Wars.

It was a fairly uneventful patrol for the first four days. Normal routine and the off-watch ratings' games of ludo – a favourite with submariners – were only interrupted once. Off Trapani an attack was made on a tanker; two of the torpedoes fired proved to be duds, and of the others only one registered a hit. Wanklyn surfaced to try and finish off the damaged tanker with his twelve-pounder, but the enemy's armament was much the stronger and he broke off the action.

The *Upholder* was still on the surface just before dawn. Her captain was on the bridge at this crucial time; the three lookouts were straining their eyes to pierce the gloom ... 'Object bearing 180 degreees!' Wanklyn swung round to look astern, focussing his night-glasses.

'All below! Dive, dive, dive!' As he tumbled down the ladder behind the lookouts he pressed the hooter, and its weird sound shrieked through the submarine.

'Up periscope.' Wanklyn squatted to follow its rise. 'Yes, an

Italian submarine,' he said, confirming his first sighting in his own mind. 'A big fellow, too – fifteen hundred tons at least, and he's got two guns.'

The Italian was more than twice the size of the *Upholder* and would certainly carry more torpedoes. In any case, Wanklyn had only one left. Speed was all-important – speed to get an attack in first. The Italian was still on the surface.

'Stand by one torpedo.' Wanklyn was grasping the periscope handles so tightly that his knuckles whitened. The range was less than a thousand yards when he gave the order 'Fire!' It had to strike – there could be no second chance.

Thirty-five seconds later he saw a flash of flame that quickly spread, and in the midst of it the target dipped and disappeared. Everyone in the *Upholder* could hear the cracking of tortured metal – to them it sounded like a matchbox being crunched up by someone standing nearby. Five minutes later the *Upholder* surfaced; Wanklyn climbed the ladder with the lookouts at his heels, and they quickly scanned the greasy patch of sea where their victim had disappeared. Three heads were bobbing about in the scum. It was dangerous for the *Upholder* to stay surfaced for long; day was breaking and she was in enemy waters, and that spread of flame must surely have been seen, would bring a swift attack from the air at any moment. But humanity prevailed; the three oil-soaked Italians were picked out of the sea – one was unconscious and had to be lowered down the hatchway on a rope – and then the *Upholder* dived from sight after an anxious fifteen minutes of seeming very conspicuous and vulnerable.

The three survivors were given dry clothes and hot drinks, and from them Wanklyn learnt that he had sunk the *Ammiraglio St Bon* which had been on passage to Palermo for repairs. One of the Italians was an officer, and he told Wanklyn that they had spotted the *Upholder* and were about to fire their gun at her when she dived. Wanklyn's uncanny sense of timing had saved them all and had removed a deadly threat to many British ships and seamen. He and his crew had started the New Year with a vengeance.

They had only six days ashore in Malta before setting out on *Upholder*'s twenty-first patrol. Her billet was just outside the Gulf of Taranto, where she would patrol in conjunction with two other submarines. A large British convoy was on its way from Alexandria to beleaguered Malta, and the three submarines had orders to prevent a sortie on it by warships from the naval base at Taranto. For several days the *Upholder* and the other two, about ten miles apart, kept guard on the mouth of the Gulf. But the expected naval force was not seen and they were recalled to Malta.

The constant strain was beginning to tell on Wanklyn. He was driving himself unmercifully and the tiredness was evident on his face. The commander of the Malta Submarine Flotilla, Captain Simpson, who had known Wanklyn for many years, proposed sending him on leave to Britain; but he refused, although he had not seen his wife and child for more than a year. However, Simpson insisted on his standing off one patrol, so when the *Upholder* next went to sea her Number One, Lieutenant G.P.Norman, was in command. She had to be kept active; combatant submarines were in short supply in the Mediterranean. So were the men to man them; and at that time the survival chances of a submarine officer or rating in the Mediterranean were put at less than even money.

Norman proved himself a worthy disciple of the master submariner. Despite much enemy air-activity he sank a merchantship and then cleverly evaded the attacks of the attendant destroyer, which tried hard for more than an hour to shatter the submarine with depth-charges. When the destroyer stopped, listening hard, the *Upholder* stopped too and Norman ordered 'silent routine'. When the destroyer speeded up for a fresh attack, he altered course and went deeper.

Depth-charges clanged like thunder and the submarine bucked and plunged. Then more waiting, with thumping hearts . . . hope rising and falling with the asdic reports: 'HE (hydrophone effect) moving up the starboard side . . . HE decreasing on Red 130.' And at last the destroyer broke off the attack and made off at speed; perhaps she had used up all her depth-charges and feared her prey's torpedoes. Norman had won the cat-and-mouse game and brought the *Upholder* safely back to her moorings in Lazaretto Creek.

On 18 March 1942 the *Upholder* was prowling around the approaches to Brindisi. In fourteen months of almost constant activity she had accounted for more ennemy shipping than any other British submarine, and the busy waters off Brindisi promised more targets. The crew were already at action stations when their captain announced, 'One merchant vessel, one escort, two aircraft'. Through the periscope he could see the merchantman zigzagging along the cleared channel, making for harbour. But he decided against attacking her; there was such a shortage of torpedoes that it was no longer good policy to shoot at every transport that came in sight. And half-an-hour later he was rewarded by the appearance of much bigger game.

'Down periscope. Stand by all tubes.' For the benefit of the crew, Wanklyn added, 'One submarine up top, steering 185 degrees. Settembrini-class submarine.'

The word was passed along and the men smiled grimly at one another. 'Good old Wanks. He knows where to find 'em.'

The attack began to take shape. 'Up periscope.' Wanklyn stroked his beard thoughtfully as he concentrated on the speed and the nature of the enemy submarine's zigzagging.

'Set torpedoes to run at eight feet,' ordered Wanklyn, having noted that the target was at full buoyancy.

'Down periscope, fifty feet.' Some sailing craft were entering the area, and Wanklyn had to manoeuvre into an attacking position without causing suspicious ripples to appear on the surface. When the periscope was raised again the Italian submarine was fairly in his sights and within six hundred yards range.

'Fire one.' The *Upholder* shivered and lifted slightly. 'Fire two,' Wanklyn ordered eight seconds later, his eye glued to the periscope. While Norman deftly maintained the submarine at a steady depth, two more torpedoes streaked from her tubes at eight seconds' interval. As the fourth was fired, a stunning crash shook the *Upholder* – the first torpedo had ripped into the Italian's hull. Then the second struck the stern, and water and debris shot skywards in a belch of smoke. When it cleared there was no sign of the submarine.

The *Upholder* went deep and hurried away. It would have been folly to surface and search for survivors; already an assortment of torpedo-boats and other submarine-chasers were speeding out of harbour towards the scene of disaster.

Before nightfall the *Upholder*'s empty torpedo-tubes were reloaded while at a depth of fifty feet, for handling heavy torpedoes in a limited space was always a tricky task and the slightest roll or pitch could lead to a fatal accident. The sweating torpedo-party hoped that their labours had not been in vain – the first four missiles had done their deadly work well, but some torpedoes now being supplied were very ancient and might have deteriorated from long storage. Submarines operating out of besieged Malta, however, had to be content with whatever the dockyard could produce.

When darkness had fallen the *Upholder* surfaced to recharge her batteries and ventilate the interior. A few at a time, the crew were able to go up top, the fresh night air striking dizzily at their starved lungs; then came the luxurious moment of lighting a cigarette. Morning found Wanklyn and his company ready for action again, cruising at periscope depth in coastal waters. But except for surfacing to shell and sink a trawler – unworthy of a precious torpedo – the next few days were unproductive of victims.

A south-east gale blew up, lashing the waters off the heel of Italy into a frothing fury. Rain fell heavily too, reducing visibility almost to nil. The *Upholder* was rolling and pitching so much that all the skill of her Number One and the men at the hydroplanes could not keep her steady at periscope depth, and to steer a straight course was beyond any helmsman's capabilities.

'Diving stations! Stand by all tubes!'

Wanklyn had vaguely sighted something big; a few minutes later, while the *Upholder* was threatening to break surface at any moment in that blustering sea, he identified the bridge and funnels of an Italian battleship. He managed to get into an attacking position at four thousand yards range, and in the worst possible conditions ordered, 'Fire all tubes!' Miraculously the submarine did not break surface. 'Down periscope. Sixty feet.' Even at that depth she still rolled alarmingly. Nearly everyone had his eyes on a watch or a clock . . . the seconds and the minutes ticked past until it was obvious that no thundering 'crump' was to be their reward. They had done their best, but that was poor consolation.

One useful thing could still be done. The *Upholder* surfaced and a message was sent to Malta reporting the whereabouts of the battleship. Then a course was laid for home, and a rough, most unpleasant passage it was, with many of even that hard-bitten crew seasick for much of the time.

On her return to base *Upholder*'s crew were given a ten-day rest period before leaving on her twenty-fifth patrol. Lieutenant Norman was transferred to another submarine and his place as Number One was taken by Lieutenant P.R.Allen. Petty Officer Selby also left the *Upholder*, having been promoted Chief Petty Officer. But when she sailed again, on 6 April

1942, most of the crew had shared in the majority of her exploits; and, like her captain, quite a few had not seen their wives and families for sixteen months or more.

There were three passengers on board, for this time the *Upholder* was engaged on another 'cloak-and-dagger' affair. When Wanklyn read the contents of the envelope marked 'Confidential, not to be opened until at sea', he found that his chief duty was to ensure the success of the 'Special Operations' landing in the control of Captain R. Wilson; on its completion he was to transfer the army captain to the submarine *Unbeaten*, west of Lampion Rock, and then proceed southward to patrol the western approaches to Tripoli.

Captain 'Tug' Wilson was an old friend of Wanklyn and of several other submarine commanders; he had made many daring landings from submarines to commit sabotage of enemy communications. While waiting at Malta for passage home for a well-deserved leave he had been asked to carry out one more task, to put two North African Arabs ashore with their radio-transmitters. The mission of these two agents was to send back information about sailings from North African ports in enemy hands. Wilson had agreed, and his transfer to the *Unbeaten* was arranged so that he could be taken to Gibraltar and proceed on leave from there.

On the night of 9 April the *Upholder* surfaced off the hostile coast, went close inshore and stopped motors. There was no moon and the only sound was the beating of the surf. Wanklyn and the lookouts manned the bridge and inspected the darkness for a few minutes. Then word was passed down to Wilson; his collapsible canoe and inflatable dinghy were hauled up the hatchway and got ready by some of the crew. The submarine's main vents were opened so that she settled lower in the water; canoe and dinghy were launched, and when Wilson and his two Arabs came up top they were able to step easily into them from the casing.

'Good luck, Tug,' said Wanklyn softly. 'Mind how you go.'

The two craft headed for the shore, Wilson paddling the canoe and towing the dinghy holding the two agents and their equipment. Wanklyn waited anxiously, hoping that the frail craft would get safely through the surf and that the shore was deserted. Less than an hour later Wilson was back, alone. 'Operation successful.' His canoe was stowed inboard and the *Upholder* moved off to deeper, safer waters.

Twenty-four hours later contact was made with the *Unbeaten*, and in the grey dawn of 11 April the two submarines closed in towards each other on the surface. Wilson joined Wanklyn on the bridge. The sea was whipping up a little.

'Doesn't look too good, Tug,' said Wanklyn half-jokingly. 'Why not finish the patrol with me? You can fly home from Malta.'

Wilson obviously thought he would get home more quickly from Gibraltar. 'Much as I love your company, David, I'll cross over to her and take my chance.'

As he paddled his canoe across to the *Unbeaten* her First Lieutenant called to him, 'Go back, Tug. We've two feet of water in the fore-ends. We'll never make it to Gib.'

Fortunately Wilson was used to these heavy naval jests, otherwise he might have stayed aboard the *Upholder*. . . .

Wanklyn set a course to his patrol area west of Tripoli and the following afternoon he received orders from base to establish a patrol line in conjunction with two other submarines, the *Urge* and *Thrasher*, to intercept a convoy bound for Tripoli on 15 April. Wanklyn acknowledged the signal, and that was the last ever heard of him and his crew.

On the afternoon of the 14th the crew of the *Thrasher*, next in line to the *Upholder*, heard the din of prolonged depth-charging. Later in the day the *Thrasher* made contact with the

Urge but could get no reply from the *Upholder*. She had made her last dive, and her gallant commander and crew had joined the far too numerous company of 'Submarines still on patrol.'

10 The Attack on the 'Lonesome Queen', September 1943

An odd little submersible was being tried out in a steep-banked stretch of Loch Striven, off the Clyde, in October 1942. The commander, Lieutenant Donald Cameron, had been in big submarines and now found that the accommodation for him and his crew of two was rather like living in a cubby-hole under the stairs. This was a midget submarine, the *X-3*, so numbered because *X-1* had been an experimental giant submarine that was scrapped as impracticable, and *X-2* had been a captured enemy vessel. The length of *X-3* was a little under fifty feet, but the actual living-space for the crew was only thirty-five feet, about half the length of a cricket-pitch; and there was barely five feet of head-room. Three more X-craft became available for training before the end of the year, and a few months later six midget submarines and their crews began working up for an attack on the big German warships anchored in a Norwegian fjord.

The development of a midget submarine as a weapon to attack an enemy fleet in harbour had been stepped up after the success of the Italian 'human torpedoes' in Alexandria harbour. A memo from Churchill had speeded progress on the *X-3* which had been on the stocks for the best part of three years; scientists and technicians, diving instructors and senior submarine officers had all pressed the project forward, overcoming innumerable difficulties and problems.

The crews were all volunteers, many from the navies of the Commonwealth, young men in their early twenties of first-class physique and with high personal qualities of courage, determination and self-control. They were going to need all that, as well as technical ability and great stamina. They had been rigorously selected from the large number of officers and ratings who had volunteered for 'special service' without any idea of their destiny. Even training activities were dangerous; by May 1943 two officers had lost their lives underwater, and Loch Striven had been the scene of several near-fatal accidents.

The craft was a complete submarine in miniature, except for the torpedo-tubes. The armament consisted instead of two explosive charges housed externally on either side of the hull; each contained two tons of amatol explosive and a time-clock, and was meant to be left on the bottom, beneath the hull of the target. The six operational X-craft, numbers 5 to 10, had a modified interior layout but were no larger in size than the *X-3*. And a fourth member had been added to each crew, a specially trained diver, often an ex-charioteer. Charioteers were the British equivalent of the Italian human torpedoes and some had already taken part in offensive operations, including a brave but unsuccessful attempt in late October 1942 to reach and damage the *Tirpitz*.

An X-craft had a maximum surface speed of six knots on the diesel engines and could dive for thirty-six hours on the batteries. The crew of four worked in two watches, four hours on and four off. When at action stations the captain did the chart work and conned the submarine by occasional glimpses through the periscope; the Number One was at the main motor and hydroplanes; the third hand, who was generally an officer but sometimes a rating, was dressed for diving with his oxygen breathing-bag on and ready, except for the face-piece;

the Engine-room Artificer was in general charge of all machinery but also lent the other three a hand and relieved the diver when he left the craft to cut a way through anti-submarine nets or to fix an explosive charge to the target's bottom.

In the spring of 1943 the six operational X-craft and their depot-ship moved up to Loch Cairnbawn in north-west Scotland, and all X-craft and chariots became the Twelfth Submarine Flotilla under the command of Captain W.E. Banks. The operation against the German warships was put back to the early autumn because several problems had still to be solved and the nights were getting shorter, especially in those northern latitudes. The operational crews continued to extend their experience with their craft, practising net-cutting, making mock attacks, carrying out navigational, towing and escape exercises. At the same time RAF planes based in Russia were making photographic surveys of the Altenfjord area, where the German capital ships *Tirpitz*, *Lützow* and *Scharnhorst* were lying, and the Norwegian underground was sending back reports. By late August the planning staff of Flag Officer Submarines had fixed the date of the operation and six ocean-going submarines had arrived in Loch Cairnbawn. Their task was to tow the midgets (manned by passage-crews) twelve hundred miles to the approaches to the target area, just below the North Cape, slip them and then patrol and wait to tow them back again – if any survived to be towed back. The midgets' crews would travel in the big submarines and take over from the passage-crews off the coast of Norway. All they would have to do then was to penetrate the minefields, escape detection and get through the anti-submarine nets at the entrance to the fjord, proceed sixty miles up to the head of Altenfjord, cut through the anti-torpedo nets surrounding their target, position their explosive charges for maximum damage, and return the way they had come to rendezvous with the parent submarines.

A few days before departure date all commanding officers were fully briefed by a staff officer who had flown up from London, but the specific target for each midget submarine was not then given. It was clear, however, that the chief target was the 40,000-ton battleship *Tirpitz*. This camouflaged colossus was the most dangerous warship in the world. Although the 'Lonesome Queen', as the Norwegians called her, had spent almost her entire career in Norwegian harbours, emerging briefly to threaten the Murmansk convoys and once to bombard Spitzbergen, her mere presence in the north influenced the balance of sea power. Since March 1943 she had been hiding away – except for the sortie to bombard Spitzbergen – with her consorts in the depths of Altenfjord, on latitude seventy, out of range of RAF heavy bombers and inaccessible to normal-sized submarines. Fuel was so short that she was able to sail for brief trials and gunnery practice only about twice a month, yet she was still greatly affecting the war and the disposition of British capital ships. To put the 'Lonesome Queen' definitely out of action would be a major naval victory.

The long haul began on 11 September. First away was the *X-6*, whose operational captain was one of the pioneers, Lieutenant Donald Cameron; she was in tow of the submarine *Truculent*. The other five X-craft followed, each at the end of a nylon towing-rope which was reputed to contain enough nylon for eighty thousand pairs of stockings! The passage-crews had the worst of it during the long crossing. Their task was to maintain the craft and hand her over to the operational crew in the highest state of efficiency – this after more than a week of living continuously in those cramped conditions and submerged for twenty-three hours out of every twenty-four. The midgets were kept out of sight and only surfaced to ventilate for about fifteen minutes four times a day, whereas the towing submarines stayed up top for the whole of each night and part of the day.

Final orders for Operation Source were radioed to the six submarines on the fifth day out. The *X-5*, *X-6* and *X-7* were to attack the *Tirpitz*, the *X-8* the *Lützow*, and the *X-9* and *X-10* the battle-cruiser *Scharnhorst*. On the fifth day, too, the weather deteriorated and the rough seas made towing a nightmare. One midget, the *X-9*, broke adrift and foundered with all hands. Her parent submarine, the *Syrtis*, did not know the tow-rope had parted until the time came for the midget to surface for the periodic fifteen minutes. The *Syrtis* turned and retraced the previous hours' track, but neither she nor any of the other submarines ever sighted the *X-9* again.

That same morning another midget, the *X-8*, found that the tow had parted. The crew succeeded in blowing the main ballast-tanks in time, but when the captain, Lieutenant J. Smart, clambered out on to the casing there was no sign of the *Seanymph*, the towing submarine. Smart decided to plough along on his own in the hope of being picked up. And, by a fantastic chance, soon after 17.00 hours he did sight a submarine – not the *Seanymph* but the *Stubborn* with the *X-7* in tow, running a little behind schedule. The *Stubborn* kept company with the *X-8* and made a signal to Admiral Submarines to be passed to the *Seanymph*. But just before midnight, in the turmoil of sea and wind, the *X-8* lost contact with the *Stubborn* and was on her own again. Fortunately the *Stubborn* sighted the *Seanymph* about three hours later and gave her the errant midget's approximate position. For most of that day, 16 September, Smart and his crew were alone in their tiny craft on the heaving waters just below the Arctic Circle, valiantly plugging on towards Norway. When the *Seanymph* at last hove in sight they were bone weary; the operational crew relieved them and took over the tow. But the vicissitudes of the *X-8* were not over. She developed a number of mechanical faults; first one and then the other explosive charge had to be jettisoned, and the force of the detonation of the second caused so much damage to the midget that it was decided to scuttle her. Intense disappointment was felt by all on board the *Seanymph*, especially by the *X-8*'s operational crew, when she was left with a subsidiary role of patrolling off the Norwegian coast.

Sea conditions continued 'rough to very rough', but the remaining four midgets were successfully towed to the approaches to Altenfjord, and on the night of the nineteenth their operational crews transferred to them. The attack plan had not been altered because of the loss of the *X-8* and *X-9*, which meant that only one midget, the *X-10*, would attack the *Scharnhorst*; but the three intended for the major target, the *Tirpitz*, were very much present and their young crews were full of confidence. They formed a friendly, cohesive band of brothers, with officers and ratings on Christian-name terms when no outsiders were around, a private little navy determined to prove their worth in this first venture of a new offensive arm. The midgets had been well maintained during the passage. 'The crew had left the craft in A-one condition,' said Sub-Lieutenant Lorimer of the *X-6*'s operational crew. 'How they stood eight days being towed in that confined space, I've no idea. It must have been very grim.' And Lieutenant Godfrey Place, the *X-7*'s captain, said that the passage-crew could not have done their job better. The little force had made its landfall undetected, no mean feat for six large and four small submarines, and a great temptation had to be resisted when a U-boat was sighted on the surface and passed within 1,500 yards range of the submerged *Syrtis*. But operational orders strictly forbade an attack on anything less than a capital ship while on passage or in the patrol area.

On 20 September the four midgets set off independently to cross the minefield and reach Altenfjord, while the six parent submarines withdrew to seaward. Lorimer, *X-6*'s Number One, found getting a trim rather difficult, probably due to layers of fresh water, but 'we had an uneventful passage across the minefield during the night, and successfully made our way up Altenfjord during the daylight hours.' The *X-6* spent part of the night of 21 September in the lee of a small island near the head of Altenfjord, charging her batteries, and at 01.00 hours went in to the attack. The *Tirpitz* lay deep in the narrow, cliff-lined Kaafjord, an inlet of Altenfjord; the entrance was guarded by anti-submarine nets, and the battle-ship herself was surrounded by anti-torpedo nets.

Lieutenant Cameron dived for his approach up Kaafjord, then discovered that his periscope was flooded and almost use-less. He surfaced in the wake of a small coaster and followed her undetected through the nets. Once in Kaafjord, he took the *X-6* down to sixty feet and proceeded by dead reckoning. By 07.05 he was within striking distance of his target. He passed through the anti-torpedo nets in the same audacious way, following close behind a picket-boat. When they were through, the boat-gate was closed, as Cameron just discerned on his periscope and reported to his crew. 'So we can't change our minds now,' joked ERA Goddard, at the wheel.

The water was calm and shallow, and the *X-6* ran aground. It was impossible to free her without breaking surface briefly, but long enough to be sighted from the *Tirpitz*. However, she was dismissed as a porpoise playing around, and Cameron got inside the range of the battleship's guns. Then the luck desert-ed him; when only some eighty yards abeam of his target the *X-6* got caught in an obstruction and he had to surface, this time to be greeted by small-arms fire from the deck looming above. He dived again, estimating distance and direction, and scraped along the hull of the *Tirpitz*. Despite depth-charges and hand-grenades showering down he managed to release and lay his explosive charges, set for one hour ahead, under the battleship's keel. There was no hope of escape, so he gave orders to scuttle the midget on top of the charges and to bail out. The time was 07.15.

136

The four crew – Cameron, Lorimer, Goddard and Sub-Lieutenant Kendall – were picked out of the water by one of the *Tirpitz*'s boats, taken on board the battleship and placed under guard, though they were given hot coffee and schnapps. For some reason the Germans took them to be Russians, perhaps because of their untidy beards or because of the nearness of Russian waters. They were not interrogated straight away, but obviously the Germans thought limpet mines had been laid, for divers were sent down to examine the hull. Action stations were ordered, steam was raised, and a tug was called for to help the battleship to take evasive action. Meanwhile her bow was shifted some 150 feet within the nets by heaving in on the starboard cable. Cameron and the other three, huddled together on deck, kept sneaking a look at their watches, wondering what effect the charges would have. Imagine the agony of standing there trying to look unconcerned, knowing the explosions were due at any moment by then!

Just as they were being interrogated the charges went off – four, not two.

> There was panic on board the *Tirpitz* [Kendall wrote later, after the war]. The gun-crews shot up a number of their own tankers and small boats, and also wiped out a gun position inboard with their own uncontrolled firing. Everybody seemed to be waving pistols and threatening us to find out the number of midgets on the job. The Germans lost about a hundred men all told, mostly due to their own lack of discipline.

The explosions heaved the big ship upwards five or six feet leaving her with a list to port. Men were hurled off their feet and about forty more were wounded. All the lights failed and much damage was done. The explosions also threw up the *X-7* and gunfire from the *Tirpitz* poured into her.

The *X-7* had had a rough passage up Kaafjord. She had

passed through the anti-submarine net at the entrance successfully but then got caught in some very strong anti-torpedo nets which had once housed the *Lützow*. Lieutenant Place did not want to send out his diver, Sub-Lieutenant Bob Aitken, if he could help it, especially as this was a case of getting free from a net and not of getting through one. But it took more than an hour of pumping and blowing, going ahead and then astern, to shake the midget free, and the violent action put the gyro-compass out of order and badly affected the trim-pump. Nevertheless Place was within attacking distance of the *Tirpitz* almost at the same time as the *X-6* (though without knowing this, of course), and went down to seventy-five feet to get under the nets, which had been reported by the Norwegian Resistance to be sixty feet deep. Again the *X-7* got caught up, broke clear, and tried again at ninety feet – to get stuck by the bow.

Here more difficulty in getting out was experienced [Place wrote with typical understatement in his report after the war], but after five minutes of wriggling and blowing she started to rise. The compass had gone wild and I was uncertain how close to the shore we were; so we stopped the motor, and *X-7* was allowed to come right up to the surface with very little way on. By some lucky chance we must have either passed under the nets or worked our way through the boat-passage for, on breaking surface, I could see the *Tirpitz* right ahead, with no intervening nets, and not more than thirty yards away. . . . 'Forty feet – full speed ahead.' We struck the *Tirpitz* on her port side and slid gently under the keel. There the starboard charge was released in the full shadow of the ship. 'Sixty feet – slow astern.' Then the port charge was released about 150 to 200 feet farther aft. . . . The next three-quarters of an hour were very trying. *X-7* was in and out of several nets, the air in the last bottle was soon exhausted and the compressor had to be run.

The crew had heard the enemy counter-attacking and assumed it was meant for them. But it was being directed at the *X-6*.

> . . . It was extremely annoying to run into another net at sixty feet. Shortly after this (at 08.12) there was a tremendous explosion. This evidently shook us out of the net, and when we surfaced it was tiresome to see the *Tirpitz* still afloat.

The *X-7* had become uncontrollable and more fire from the *Tirpitz* damaged the hull. Place decided to abandon ship and 'opened the fore hatch just enough to allow the waving of a white sweater. Firing stopped, so I came outside and waved the sweater more vigorously.'

Then the midget, already low in the water, bumped hard against a gunnery target some five hundred yards off the starboard bow of the *Tirpitz*, shipped water down the hatch before Place could shut it, and sank. He just had time to step on to the gunnery target before the midget went down.

Place was rescued from his precarious position by a German picket-boat and taken aboard the *Tirpitz*. He was dressed only in vest, long submarine-issue pants, with no trousers, and wearing an enormous pair of fleece-lined boots lent him by Lieutenant Philip, the South African captain of *X-7*'s passage-crew. 'He was a cheering sight,' Lorimer remembered later with some irony, 'standing shivering underneath a gun-turret.'

He was also very depressed about the possible fate of his crew and by the fact of the *Tirpitz* still being afloat. He need not have worried so much about the latter. All her main engines had been damaged, two gun-turrets were out of action, her rudder was twisted and there were massive equipment failures. The battleship had in fact been put out of action for many months.

Before the Germans had time to assess all this damage another midget was sighted outside the nets, about half-an-hour after the explosions. This was the *X-5*, commanded by Lieutenant H. Henty-Creer. The *Tirpitz*'s light guns opened fire on her and obtained several hits; she disappeared, and depth-charges were dropped over the spot. Nothing more was ever seen of her and her crew.

More than two hours later, after Place and the *X-6* crew had been put in the cells, Sub-Lieutenant Aitken bobbed up in the water, barely conscious, and was picked up by a German boat just in time. He had escaped from the sunken *X-7* using a DSEA set, but it had been a very near thing. The midget had settled on the bottom at a depth of 120 feet; the hatch had been shut in time, and the boat was more or less dry. All three men put on escape sets, went through the drill, and started to flood the craft. It was much too slow a process, for only one small hull valve could be got open to let in the water; all the others had jammed, probably due to the explosion. The air got worse; the icy water was above their waists but still not high enough for the pressure within to equal the pressure without. Then the water had reached an electric circuit, the boat began to fill with fumes, and the three men were forced to start breathing their escape-oxygen. Before the escape hatch could be opened they were on to their individual emergency supply-cylinders. And only Aitken had managed to hang on long enough to make his escape. With little more breath than what he held in his lungs he had pushed desperately to open the hatch and then blacked out, coming to again as he broke surface.

While all this heroism and tragedy and damage to the enemy was being enacted, the fourth midget was lying on the bottom in 195 feet of water at the head of Altenfjord with her

140

crew striving to repair the defects that had developed. Her captain was an Australian, Lieutenant Ken Hudspeth, and her diver, Sub-Lieutenant G.Harding, was the youngest person taking part in Operation Source, being just over nineteen. The compass was wandering, the depth-gauge was not functioning properly, and the periscope hoisting-motor had burnt out. Sub-Lieutenant B. Enzer, the Number One, had lashed the periscope in a raised position and hung a sharp knife close at hand. The arrangement had been quickly named the Enzer Periscope Motor – 'To lower, cut the cord and stand clear.'

They heard the explosive charges go off, at the exact time as laid down in the operational instructions, and were much cheered by this.

We stayed on the bottom all that day [young Harding related afterwards], and I think we were all feeling very mixed inside. We were glad about the bangs, but sad that they weren't ours. We were glad that we didn't *have* to take our wreck of a boat in to attack, but sad because it was a wreck of a boat by this time and could not really make an attack.

By 18.00 hours we had been on the bottom nearly sixteen hours. Early on we had worked on some of the defects, but for the last few hours we had just been lying still and waiting for a good time to get away. The air we were breathing was getting worse every hour. . . .

Hudspeth finally decided to abandon their attack on the *Scharnhorst.* This was just as well, for it was discovered later that the battle-cruiser was away from her anchorage at the time. On the night of the twenty-second Hudspeth surfaced and conned the *X-10* back down the fjord, and two days later reached one of the rendezvous positions. He waited three nights, but no submarine showed up, so he decided to try elsewhere:

> We planned to make for Iceland or Russia if we made no contact with a submarine that night. We patrolled close inshore all during that evening and into the night. Just after midnight Ken announced that we would give up waiting in another hour's time exactly. There was a large amount of quietness aboard. . . .

About five minutes before the hour was up a submarine was seen closing the shore. She was the *Stubborn*, which had towed the *X-7* across. She and the other five submarines had been waiting off the coast for six days; they waited one day more, then started the return journey, with the *Stubborn* towing the one midget. And this surviving craft was scuttled when halfway to the Shetlands, on orders from base; a gale was imminent in the area and there was no point in risking the lives of the midget's crew.

Nine men had been lost in the operation, which had proved the offensive ability of midget submarines when crewed by brave men and had eliminated the 40,000-ton *Tirpitz* as an effective force. It took seven months to repair her where she lay, by seven hundred men sent from Germany, and then she was able only to limp from her anchorage and reach Tromso, where she was finally sunk by Bomber Command in November 1944.

The six survivors of the three-midget attack were well treated aboard their victim, where their bravery was greatly admired. They ended the war as POWs in Germany. Cameron and Place were both awarded the Victoria Cross, and the other four received high decorations. Hudspeth was awarded the DSC for his part, and later a bar to it for his sterling work in command of one of the two midgets which acted as markers off the Normandy coast for the D-Day landings. And midget submarines continued to prove their worth after the war in Europe had ended. . . .

11 Last out of La Pallice, September 1944

In early August 1944 a U-boat captain was training his men to fight as infantry in the defence of Brest. Their *U-415* had struck a magnetic mine in the harbour a few days before and had sunk with several of the crew. Now Oberleutnant Herbert Werner was wondering whether he would ever get to sea again. Thirteen of the fifteen U-boats which had been based at Brest before the Allied invasion of Normandy in June were known to be lost at sea, and the remaining two – the *U-953* and *U-247* – were awaiting repairs in the concrete bunkers. Werner and his men seemed more likely to be killed or captured on land by the Allied forces encircling Brest. More American tanks supported by French Resistance fighters were rolling south, cutting across Brittany to isolate the other submarine bases at Lorient and St Nazaire. At sea, British destroyers were blockading the exits while Allied aircraft were dropping mines in the coastal waters and bombing the port installations. The ring was tightening around the French Atlantic ports which had once been the bases of a successful fleet of several hundred U-boats but were now sheltering just a few lame ones in bunkers made of concrete more than twenty feet thick.

One evening as Werner was returning from field exercises with his submariners he received word to report to Korvetten-Kapitan Winter, the commander of what was left of the First

144

U-boat Flotilla. He hurried up to the Naval College where Winter had his headquarters, wondering what was in store for him. Werner was only twenty-four and life was sweet; he had been serving in ocean-going U-boats for more than three years and had fought in many seas; he had lived through the rise and fall of the U-boat force, and had learnt of the death of nearly all his friends and colleagues in the service.

His commander had a surprise for him. 'You're a lucky man, Werner. You have been appointed to the command of *U-953*. Congratulations.'

Her captain had been called to Berlin to receive the Knight's Cross, as Werner knew, and the Allied advance had prevented his return to Brest.

'Repairs to the *U-953* will be completed in about ten days,' Winter added. 'Then you'll have an exciting task.'

When Werner went down to take over his new command he found that some of the crew had gone on leave a week or two before; and, like their ex-captain, the rapidity of the Allied advance would prevent them from rejoining. So Werner filled their places with members of the crew of his late command; they, like him, were overjoyed at the prospect of getting away to sea and continuing the fight in the way they had been trained.

There was much to be done to the *U-953* to make her sea-worthy and a fighting unit again. The French dockyard work-ers disappeared or were openly hostile and more ready to commit sabotage; the German technicians were more inter-ested in escaping from Fortress Brest, as it was now named, and offered large bribes to be smuggled aboard the *U-953* when she made her escape. Most of the repairs had to be done by the U-boat's own engineers with what little material was available, and the work took longer than expected.

Meanwhile there was fighting in the suburbs and American tanks broke in at several points. The city was being defended by scratch units made up of naval personnel, garrison clerks and army stragglers, with headquarters in the tunnels under the old Naval College. A strict curfew had been imposed upon the civilians, who spent much of the time in their cellars. Between 9 and 13 August heavy bomber formations repeatedly attacked the gun positions and the submarine pens. On the thirteenth six-ton bombs scored direct hits on the pens where the two remaining U-boats were being repaired.

As soon as the raid was over, Werner hurried down to inspect the damage. There was just one hole thirty feet across in the thickly reinforced roof, and the *U-953* was covered with a fine layer of cement dust. A torpedo tube door had been blown in, but that was from the blast of another bomb and was the only damage to either of the U-boats. Werner gave a sigh of relief and urged the chief engineer to press on with the work.

The other U-boat was ready for sea first, but when she made her break was sunk with all her complement just outside the narrows leading from Brest. Werner received his final orders a few days later. He was to make for La Pallice, the naval base one hundred miles south of the mouth of the Loire. The Allied armoured divisions had swung east along that river, speeding to trap the German forces fighting desperately in Lower Normandy. It was still thought possible for Germans to make their way across the southern half of France, despite the growing strength and activity of the Resistance groups. The *U-953* was to be loaded with valuable engineering equipment and instruments and to take a number of key technicians on board.

Werner collected as many of his old crew as he could from the perimeter defences and sent them aboard to join the *U-953*'s crew; altogether this made a complement of ninety-two. When he himself went aboard he found six civilians waiting on the bridge, all with signed orders to sail with him. On the quayside was a large, noisy group of civilians, French col-

laborators and Germans, all wanting to leave on the U-boat.
Werner mustered his men and addressed them in a loud
voice for everyone's benefit:

> I want you to know that the coastal waters are crawling
> with enemy ships and our chances of surviving are very
> poor. It's ten-to-one against us breaking through and reach-
> ing La Pallice, so don't have any illusions. The regular crew
> will maintain the controls while the crew of *U-415* will help
> with their normal jobs. You'll remain at action stations the
> whole time. You must be prepared for instant sailing. I
> want to emphasize that this patrol will be one of our hard-
> est.

Werner dismissed the men and turned to the six civilians,
and to his secret satisfaction he saw two of them looking fear-
fully dismayed; they picked up their luggage and hurried
ashore, evidently preferring the devil they knew, despite their
orders to escape by sea. Werner took the remaining four below
and found a place for them in the forward torpedo-
compartment which, like everywhere else in the boat except
the control-room, was piled with crates and boxes and pack-
ages. He left them looking bewildered and apprehensive, and
went to report to Winter that he was ready to sail, although
the diesels were in poor condition and the batteries should
have been replaced – but there were no others available.
However, Winter told him to postpone sailing for twenty-four
hours as four more indispensable technicians were being sent
to join him. Werner returned fuming to his U-boat; every
delay made it harder to break through the enemy blockade
and reach La Pallice.

Finally the *U-953* slid from her berth at 21.30 on 22
August, in the middle of an air-raid which smashed the
Naval College into rubble. While ack-ack guns barked
furiously and bombs exploded on Fortress Brest, Werner

took the U-boat cautiously and noiselessly – so as not to acti-
vate any acoustic mines – to the middle of the roadstead and
then submerged for his chief engineer to catch a trim. It took
more than an hour, for the weight of the cargo and its uneven
distribution created unusual problems. Moreover, there were
one hundred and one men on board – the normal complement
was forty-four.

It was all to no purpose; they were back in port before the
night was over, driven back by a dozen or so British MTBs
lurking outside the narrows. Werner decided to try again at
high tide, when he might be able to make a submerged exit.
Dawn was streaking the sky as he headed seaward again. The
MTBs were still lying in wait and they sighted the U-boat
before she reached water deep enough to submerge. Then she
crept over the sandy bottom, frequently changing course,
being repeatedly depth-charged, until she glided into the Bay
of Biscay and turned on a south-easterly course, out of the
trap.

Fortunately the *U-953* was equipped with a *schnörkel*, or
snort, a collapsible air-mast which allowed her to use her diesels while submerged and to recharge batteries. It also drew
cool sea air into the compartments, which was a blessed relief
to the hundred men when Werner had the mast erected that
night.

At dawn on 26 August Werner poked up his periscope and
made out a thin, broken line to the east – the two islands of Ré
and Oléron which he had to pass between to reach La Pallice.
But now these waters were being patrolled by enemy destroyers and mined by aircraft. Three U-boats had been sunk in the
approaches a few days before. Even as Werner scanned the
area he saw a flight of enemy planes come into view at low alti-
tude. He downed the periscope and rested on the sea-bottom
all that day. When darkness fell he surfaced, took several bear-
ings on a lighthouse and began his run in to port. But he had

mistaken the lighthouse on the Ile de Ré for the one on Oléron, and found himself running aground; during the day he had unknowingly been carried north by the strong current. However, he had also been carried past the mined area; and the following night, having plotted his position off the coast, he reached the channel into La Pallice and was escorted in by a minesweeper, while shadowy British destroyers were weaving inquiringly to seaward. In the early hours of 28 August the *U-953* glided into a berth in the concrete bunker. She was the only U-boat to reach La Pallice from the bases at Brest, Lorient and St Nazaire.

In the morning Werner went into the old walled seaport of La Rochelle to report to the commander of the Third U-boat Flotilla – who had little left to command – and was told to be prepared to sail on patrol in four days' time. His cargo would be loaded on to army lorries and taken to Germany, and his supernumeraries would be repatriated. The commander must have been a very optimistic man or, more probably, unaware of the true military situation in France.

Werner protested that his batteries and diesels needed replacing.

'We have no supplies here,' he was told. 'You will have to wait for replacements until you get to Norway.'

The crew of the *U-953* worked frantically to get her into fighting condition in time, but it was a week before the chief engineer could report her ready – with several provisos. In the meantime a motley army of some twenty-five thousand Germans had tried to escape eastward from the La Rochelle area, across a France in a state of wild confusion; most of them were either killed or captured. The Allies had landed on the coast of provence and their armoured divisions were heading up the Rhône valley to make juncture with the liberating armies in the north. Paris had been freed on 24 August. The demoralized Germans in the west were ambushed by French

Resistance groups, were bombed and machine-gunned by Allied aircraft, and with their supply and communication lines cut surrendered by the thousand. La Rochelle held out, now isolated by French Forces of the Interior who gradually tightened the ring. Even in the town itself no German was safe. Werner and his crew, like every other unit, locked themselves in their temporary billet and posted sentries when night fell. One morning two naval officers were found in a side street stripped almost naked, their throats slit and penises cut off. Despite the chief engineer's provisos, the crew of the *U-953* were only too glad to have a chance of escaping from the doomed garrison. They were no better off in La Rochelle than they had been in Brest.

The one other seaworthy U-boat in the pens at La Pallice, the *U-260*, had sailed at the end of August and succeeded in breaking through the blockade (though she later struck a mine when off the south coast of Ireland). This left the *U-953* the only occupant of the vast concrete bunkers which had once housed more than forty U-boats. She was in fact the last U-boat to lay in any French port. Those at Bordeaux had sailed for Norway at the end of August, except four which were blown up because no new batteries could be provided for them.

When Werner reported on 6 September that he was ready to sail he was told that the Senior Officer U-boats West wanted to see him. He found this officer, Kapitan Rösing, at a large house where there were many signs of confusion and imminent departure; marines were burning piles of documents on the lawn, officers were coming and going, and orderlies were loading equipment and luggage on to an assortment of vehicles, civilian and military.

Rösing interrupted his packing to hand Werner some charts and data on enemy minefields and to give him orders to patrol in the North Channel, between the coast of northern Ireland

and the minefields west of Scotland – if he could get there. He would receive operational details from Dönitz's Headquarters while at sea.

Werner spent the French money remaining in his pockets while on the way back to La Pallice, buying a housecoat for his mother and some silk stockings for his sister. He had earlier given his crew time off to go shopping, and had recommended his First Lieutenant to buy all the fresh vegetables he could get.

When Werner reached his U-boat he found the First Lieutenant supervising the loading of food supplies. 'We sail one hour after midnight,' he told him. 'Without an escort, but keep that to yourself. We'll leave as quietly as possible.'

It was a bitter moment for him, a U-boat captain who had known the triumphant days of the Battle of the Atlantic, when the *U-953* crept from its lair – the last U-boat to sail from the last Biscay port still being operated by the Germans. But he felt better when his skilful handling had enabled the U-boat to elude the enemy destroyers standing off the coast. As the stars faded and day began to dawn the watchdogs withdrew seaward, out of range of the coastal batteries, and the *U-953* chugged southwards on her worn-out engines, keeping close to the shore, then rounded the Ile d'Oléron and headed out to sea.

A storm blew up late on the second day and made use of the snort difficult. If the boat dipped under the heavy sea, the snort valve closed automatically and at once the diesels sucked all the air out of the boat, creating a vacuum which took the crew's breath away and made their heads feel about to burst. However, in such a sea radar detection of the snort head and the periscope was almost impossible, compensating for the unpleasant side-effects of use of the snort.

A signal was received from U-boat Headquarters ordering the *U-953* to take up the southern-most position on a patrol line west of the North Channel which was to be completed by three other U-boats. At the end of the transmission of tactical signals, Headquarters flashed out a brief news summary which was depressing for the submariners and particularly so for Werner. He heard of a heavy bombing raid on Darmstadt; the city centre had been wiped out and tens of thousands of people killed and injured. Darmstadt was his home town; his family lived in the centre. Personal worries were now added to his burden, nagging at his mind as he took his command north-west across the Atlantic, a lone wolf that was more hunted than hunter and seemed likely to become a cripple at any moment.

One mechanical fault was succeeded by another, and the engineers were kept busy at temporary and ingenious repairs. On the tenth day out the starboard diesel packed up, and holding the boat at snort-depth became a nerve-racking task. Then the snort went wrong; instead of drawing in air it drew in water, tons of it, and the boat plunged down at an angle. She was brought under control but the same thing happened again. Werner surfaced and, on a wild rainy night with a mountainous sea, ran in towards the Irish coast; the engineers located the trouble and effected repairs. Next to go out of order was the gyro-compass. Werner rested the boat on the sea-bottom, and this time the dismantling and re-assembling took nearly a whole day.

At last the *U-953* reached her patrol area, more than two weeks after sneaking out of La Pallice. Werner found there was much anti-submarine activity by enemy destroyers and aircraft guarding the convoy route round the north of Ireland, and he was given little opportunity to go over to the offensive. The *U-953* spent much of the time skulking on the sea-bottom, nursing her injuries. Information was received from Headquarters that the other three U-boats in the patrol area had all been sunk by the enemy. It seemed that the turn of the *U-953* would come at any time.

On 29 September, after a week of ineffectual patrolling in a U-boat that was weakened by defects, Werner was forced to break off the patrol and try to make for Norway. The snort-mast had got jammed and protruded conspicuously ten or twelve feet above the water when the boat was at periscope depth. This made it impossible to manoeuvre into an attacking position without being sighted. Werner radioed a brief coded message to Headquarters: 'No enemy traffic. Strong defence. Damages. Returning to base.'

His base was now Bergen, so he had a long way to go. Fortunately the snort had stuck while upright so it could still be used. In the second week of October the *U-953* crept furtively underwater past the Shetlands, but then she was located by a destroyer group waiting to pounce on U-boats sailing from Norway, and for more than twenty-four hours she was assailed by depth-charges. Werner eventually wriggled away and left the hideous din astern; both U-boat and crew were almost at the end of their tether, and there was still the North Sea to cross, still submerged.

They made it – just. Six weeks after slipping out of La Pallice, most of that time submerged, the *U-953* reached Norwegian coastal waters. Werner rose to periscope depth and manoeuvred to enter Bergenfjord, and just then the snort-mast collapsed on deck with a rumble and a bang.

But the *U-953* was in safe waters. She surfaced, and the crew poured out of the hatch, away from the stench they had been living in for so long. They were haggard and whitefaced and had protruding eyes, long hair and beards. They had nothing to show for their long, courageous and agonizing voyage, but they were still free men and ready to continue the fight, hopeless though it was.

12 Operation Struggle, July 1945

'There she is!' Lieutenant Ian Fraser was looking through the periscope of his midget submarine *XE-3* at his target, the 10,000-ton Japanese heavy cruiser *Takao*. She was lying in the shallow waters of Johore Strait near the causeway linking Singapore Island to the mainland, and so her guns were a menace to any Allied troops attempting to recapture Singapore by land.

Fraser let each of his crew – Sub-Lieutenant W.J.Smith, a New Zealander, ERA Charles Reed and Leading Signalman Mick Magennis, the diver – have a quick look at the *Takao* through the periscope, and then began his run in. It was two in the afternoon of 31 July 1945, a baking hot day with a calm, clear sea.

After a four-day tow from Brunei Bay, Borneo, the *XE-3* had been slipped about forty miles from where the *Takao* was lying and had made her lonely way into the busy Strait during the night and morning. The boat-gate in the anti-submarine net had been found open, and the midget had glided slowly past the guard-vessel in water that was shallow and very translucent. An alert Japanese lookout could have ruined the whole show. Now 'Operation Struggle' was reaching its critical point.

The *Takao* lay across a depression in the sea-bed in such a way that she was almost aground fore and aft at low tide, but with more water under the midships section.

Fraser's intention was to take his craft into this deeper hole – high tide had been at midday – and there fix his explosive charges and limpet mines to the cruiser's keel.

The range had narrowed to four hundred yards, with the *XE-3*'s own keel just scraping the sea-bed and her upper deck only ten feet below the surface.

'Up periscope, stand by for a last look round.' Fraser slowly swung the periscope round. 'Down periscope quick! Bloody hell! There's a boat full of Japs only forty or fifty feet away. God, I hope they didn't see us!'

Through the lens he had seen the lips of the sailors moving as they chatted away, and even had time to notice that one of them was trailing his hand in the water.

Then the midget struck the cruiser's hull a glancing blow, seeming to make enough noise to alert the whole ship's company. The depth-gauge was showing only thirteen feet, so Fraser reckoned he was too far forward along the enemy ship.

'We'll try to run down her side. Port thirty half ahead, group down.'

The motor hummed into life, but the midget did not budge. They were jammed. But after ten minutes of going forward and then astern they broke loose, and moved out for another run in. It was then 15.00 hours – a precious hour had passed all too quickly. This time Fraser succeeded in sliding into the hole and under the keel of the *Takao*. When he looked through the periscope he could see along the keel for about fifteen yards in each direction, and it was like peering into a dark cave with the *XE-3* lying across the centre of the sunlit entrance. They were resting on the bottom with the hull of the *Takao* only a foot or so above their heads. Fraser had wedged the midget rather frighteningly between a 10,000-ton cruiser and the hard sea-bed, with the prospect of being squeezed tighter as the tide ebbed.

'Come and have a look at this,' he called to the crew. They left their positions to look at the barnacles and layers of weeds on the bottom of their target. The *Takao* had been damaged by an American submarine in the Battle of Leyte Gulf in October 1944 and since limping back to her present anchorage had not moved.

'What a dirty bastard,' was one man's comment.

But time was passing and they were anxious to be away. Magennis was already in his rubber suit; he strapped on his breathing apparatus and entered the escape compartment. Reed closed the door on him and started the pumps. When Magennis came to push up the hatch he found there was not enough room between the midget and the *Takao*'s bottom for it to open fully. Undeterred, he just managed to squeeze through by deflating his breathing apparatus and exhaling. As he began unloading the limpets from the starboard container he saw there was a slight leak from his equipment, no doubt caused by his struggles to get out of the hatchway. A steady stream of bubbles was mounting to the surface, a sure signal to any observant Japanese. He could only hope.

The three inside the midget heard the limpets being bumped along the side and could imagine Magennis at his tricky task as they counted three mines taken towards the for'ard end and three towards the after end. It was sweltering inside, but they dared not start the fan because of the noise. They sat drinking orange-juice, and the wait seemed interminable. The chronometer showed nearly 16.00, four hours after high water. The rise and fall in Johore Strait is no more than eight feet, but this was quite enough for the cruiser to drop slowly and crush the midget.

Magennis's task was trickier than they knew. The foul bottom of the cruiser prevented the magnets of the limpets from sticking, and he had first to cut away festoons of weeds with his knife and then chip off the barnacles and other parasites. The angular-shaped base of the hull was no help either. And all the time there was a slow but steady leakage from his precious oxygen supply.

He stuck at it and secured all six limpets in two groups, and set the mechanism which would detonate them in six hours' time. It took him thirty minutes – to the waiting crew they seemed more like thirty days. How long did they seem to Magennis? At last he was squeezing back through the hatch in a state of near collapse, then had a difficult job to shut the lid, for his hands were badly lacerated. He could hardly operate the valves to drain down the compartment.

The other three set to work to release the port charge of four tons of amatol, each taking a turn at unscrewing the wheel in order to share the pleasure of leaving this high explosive charge under a Japanese warship. Then the empty limpet-container on the starboard side was released and they were ready to leave. But the limpet-container would not fall away. Fraser thought that movement of the midget would shake it loose.

'Group up, half ahead. Let's get to hell out of this hole!'

Smith started the fan, a blessed relief. Magennis had come through from the escape compartment and was taking off his breathing-set, still very exhausted from his efforts.

The motor had been running for some seconds but there was no sign of movement.

'Full ahead!'

Still no movement.

'Stop, full astern, group up.'

But no, they seemed to be well and truly stuck. While they were placing their lethal charges the *Takao* had settled down on them and refused to let them go.

They tried pumping the water aft and then forward, out

and then in, and just as Fraser was envisaging waiting until half-an-hour before the charges were due to go off and then abandoning ship, she began to move slowly ahead and passed right under the *Takao*'s hull. The limpet-container was dragging the midget's head round, but they were out of that dark menacing cavern and into water through which sunlight was streaming.

'Stop the motor,' ordered Fraser. 'We'll have to release that container.'

It was still holding by the securing-pins at the top and was making the midget difficult to manoeuvre. She was lying about thirty feet away from the *Takao*'s port side and in only seventeen feet of clear water.

Magennis was still in his rubber suit but had obviously not yet recovered from his ordeal. Fraser decided that the circumstances justified the commanding officer leaving the vessel for a few minutes. He knew that if anything happened to him, Smith was fully capable of getting the midget out of the Strait to rejoin the waiting parent submarine.

'I'll go and release it myself,' he said. 'Get me the spare breathing-set.'

Magennis looked reproachfully at his commanding officer. 'I'll be all right in a minute, sir. Just let me get my wind.' He was the diver, it was up to him.

They all sat quietly for a few minutes, then Magennis went back into the escape compartment armed with a huge spanner. As he opened the hatch – at least it was easier to get out from now – a stream of air bubbles went up to the surface; and Fraser, watching Magennis through the periscope, saw more bubbles shooting upwards from his breathing-set. It all added to Fraser's worries. The water was as clear as glass – supposing some sailor gazed idly down from the rail of the ship above?

Again the three sat waiting, sweating it out, not making a

sound but hearing the chronometer ticking away and an occasional clank from Magennis's spanner. Five minutes went by, five nerve-racking minutes. Magennis seemed to be making enough hammering to alert the whole Japanese navy. Then Fraser saw Magennis give the 'thumbs-up' sign; the container fell away, Magennis slid feet first back into the hatchway and closed the lid. They were free to leave.

'Starboard twenty steer O-ninety degrees half ahead group up;' Fraser ordered all in one breath.

'Aye, aye, sir!'

The return journey was comparatively uneventful, though they had all been on duty without sleep for fifty-two hours by the time they made rendezvous with the towing submarine. On 4 August they were all safely back in Brunei Bay. It was learnt later that the charges had exploded on the evening of the attack and torn a hole sixty feet by thirty in the hull of the *Takao*, put some of her guns out of action and caused other damage. But the cruiser could still bring a few of her guns to bear on the causeway. So Fraser and his crew signified willingness to take the *XE-3* back and do it all again. They were actually ready to leave, with the tow secured, when the operation was suddenly cancelled – the war was over Instead they celebrated VJ Day in no uncertain manner.

Later there was another memorable party aboard the depot ship when the award of the Victoria Cross to Fraser and Magennis was announced.

13 Two Mysterious Disappearances, 1925 and 1951

'During exercises early this morning submarine *M-1* was seen to dive in a position about fifteen miles south of Start Point. She has not been seen since. Every effort is being made to locate her and establish communication.'

This statement was issued by the Admiralty late on 12 November 1925. *M-1* was a huge, 'freak' submarine, one of three which had been built for experimental purposes a few years before. She had been fitted with a turret forward of the conning-tower to take a twelve-inch gun that weighed sixty tons. The advantages of mounting a small gun on a submarine had been proved time and again during the First World War. How much better, then, to mount a gun of such a size that it could account for almost any ship? The submarine would stalk her prey until within close range, then bob up out of the sea, fire her gun and submerge again before the enemy had time to retaliate. The gun could be elevated from inside the submarine while she was still submerged, and the tampon fitting over the muzzle could also be worked from inside; the gun was fired electrically from the periscope. On previous exercises the *M-1*'s crew had completed the whole process – rising from a depth of thirty feet, firing the gun and diving to thirty feet again – in less than one minute.

However, the gun could only fire right ahead; the submarine, as when firing a bow torpedo, had to be pointed at the target. Opinions were divided as to the suitability of the *M-1*. Some submarine staff officers said the weight of the gun would make her unstable, or that the recoil of such a large gun would send her rushing away stern first. Neither of these things had happened so far. Certainly the *M-1* dived fast, but checked as soon as the gun was entirely submerged. She had some idiosyncrasies, but her commander at the time of her disappearance, Lieutenant-Commander Carrie, was a submariner of great experience.

The exercises in which the *M-1* was taking part had begun on 9 November. In addition to practising the use of her gun, the *M-1* was cooperating with aircraft to discover the best colour a submarine should be painted to make her invisible or at least difficult to distinguish from the air when submerged; and to this end she had been painted green, while another M-boat had been painted dark blue.

A gale blew up on 11 November and the *M-1* took shelter in Plymouth Sound. Lieutenant-Commander Carrie took her to sea again soon after midnight, when the weather had improved a little; there was still a high wind and a heavy sea, but the *M-1* had operated in worse weather. She dived at dawn – never to surface again.

The mystery of her disappearance grew daily. Visibility that morning had been fairly good. The area in which she had dived was systematically patrolled by vessels equipped with hydrophones, but not a single sound was picked up that might have come from the sunken submarine. It was presumed – somewhat hastily, one would now think – that all the *M-1*'s complement had died mercifully quickly, and the C-in-C Atlantic Fleet made a signal regretting that 'it is feared that submarine *M-1* has been lost with all hands during exercises in the Channel today.'

However, the area continued to be swept and by 15 November five objects on the sea-bottom had been located, any of which might have been the *M-1*. But they were lying in 220 feet of water, a depth much too great for divers except in perfect conditions. Several naval divers volunteered to go down but were not permitted to do so; the sea was still too rough. Instead a German diver equipped with a special reinforced diving-suit, a recent German invention, was sent for; he went down to a depth of 230 feet, but failed to find the *M-1*.

Then came a report from Stockholm that a Swedish ship, the *Vidar*, had hit a submerged object shortly before eight on the morning of 12 November when fifteen miles south of Start Point and proceeding up-Channel. The master of the *Vidar* (who had heard about the *M-1* while at Kiel) said that at the time he and his chief officer had thought the ship had bumped into an old or dummy mine. They were pitching about in a heavy sea; the ship rose to a big wave after the first bump, then came down and hit something harder than before, and for a moment refused to answer her helm.

In order to make sure that there was no coincidence, at the request of the British naval attaché the *Vidar* was put in dry dock and her hull examined. Part of the stem was found to be bent and the side plating buckled; but this could have been caused by striking any obstruction at any time. Then some green paint-marks were discovered on her bottom; some of these were scraped off and sent for analysis, and proved to be of the same composition as green paint in British naval stores. This was accepted as proof that the *M-1* had been rammed by the *Vidar*. Experts considered that the *Vidar* must have just touched the submarine when she was at periscope depth, then rose to a wave, and as the wave passed the ship's bows dropped on to the submarine and split her open.

On 2 December the Admiralty announced: 'Diving

operations in connection with submarine *M-1* have been discontinued, as no positive results have been obtained. It is not considered necessary to prolong the search, as the cause of her loss has been so fully established.'

But had it? There were several questions in the minds of some naval authorities which remained unanswered. If the *Vidar* had really been involved in such a serious collision, why was so little notice of it taken at the time? Only when she had docked and her master read of the loss of the *M-1* did he consult his chief officer and look at the log and begin to wonder. The *M-1* was fitted with hydrophones – why had they not given warning of a ship in the immediate vicinity? And as it was daylight and visibility was fairly good, why was the *Vidar* not sighted through the periscope? If indeed the *M-1*'s end was due to being rammed by the *Vidar*. The submarine had been intending to engage in target practice on the day she disappeared; on previous exercises it had been found that if the barrel of her twelve-inch gun was not clear of water, the last three feet or so of the muzzle had an embarrassing tendency to follow the shell! This in itself might not cause disaster; but what other dangers could the gun cause?

In any case, the experiment was never repeated. The *M-1* was never salved. And the Admiralty has never made any further announcement as to the cause of her loss.

More than twenty-five years later another submarine sailed out into the Channel on a training exercise and mysteriously disappeared. In her case, the search went on until she was found, even though the area in which she could possibly have sunk was a very large one.

The submarine, the *Affray*, sailed from Portsmouth on the afternoon of 16 April 1951 with seventy-five men on board. In addition to her own crew, she was carrying twenty-three submarine officers under training and some Royal Marine

Commandos. Her captain's orders gave him considerable freedom of action. He was to reach the western approaches of the Channel, either submerged or on the surface, and spend three days in a wide area simulating a submarine on war patrol for the benefit of the officers under training, and at a time of his choosing was to land the Commandos in their canoes on the Cornish coast. At least, this was all that was ever divulged of the submarine's mission on this exercise.

So the *Affray* proceeded down-Channel on the surface and at about 21.00 hours made a signal that she was diving. That was the last signal she ever made; after that, she just vanished.

Every British submarine at sea in peacetime has orders to come to the surface at stated times and report herself by radio. The *Affray* was due to make her 'on the surface' signal between 08.00 and 09.00 hours the following morning, 17 April. When nothing was heard from her by 10.00 hours, Operation Submiss was set in motion. An hour later the signal 'Emergency Subsunk' cut through the routine radio chatter of the Fleet. And at once the whole resources of the C-in-C Portsmouth were deployed in an intensive effort to find and save the missing submarine and the seventy-five men in her.

The *Affray* could be anywhere between the Isle of Wight and Land's End, the south-west coast and the Channel Islands. Powerful shore radio stations had been calling her all morning without result. So the search was essentially for some sign of her presence, for a marker buoy, for survivors or even wreckage. More than forty ships were scouring the Channel; a squadron of American destroyers left Plymouth to join in the search; dozens of aircraft swept over the area; every lifeboat along the south-west coast put to sea. It was the greatest search operation ever laid on for a missing submarine. Meanwhile every provision was made for rescuing the men when found. A veritable armada of salvage ships, tugs and lifting craft was mustered and held in readiness at south coast ports.

Two German lifting craft, the most powerful in the world, were alerted. A specialist team of naval divers was flown south from Scotland. The navy's foremost expert in submarine escape, Captain W.O.Shelford, was flown home from Malta to take charge of search and salvage operations. Every available diver and salvage officer on leave was recalled. The navy's deep diving ship *Reclaim* had half her crew on leave, but she put to sea with a scratch crew. Naval and civilian hospitals were alerted, decompression chambers were made ready in case men escaped from a great depth. In fact every possible contingency was provided for and the search was pursued with a vigour and sense of urgency which had been sadly lacking in the case of the *Thetis*.

The search for the *Affray* went on for more than two days without the slightest trace of her being found. The only helpful clue, a somewhat negative one, was that the Marines had never been landed on the Cornish beach. On the evening of 19 April it was announced that all hope of saving life from the *Affray* had been abandoned. The ships and aircraft and lifeboats were recalled; the salvage vessels and tugs, the divers and doctors were dispersed. But the search for the wreck continued, under the direction of Captain Shelford. This time the Admiralty seemed determined to discover the cause of the disaster; there was also the pressure of public opinion, for the mass media had roused people's imagination.

The probable area in which the *Affray* was lying extended over 1,500 square miles – one of the biggest graveyards of shipping in the world, and notorious for its fogs and gales. Searching for the *Affray* was like looking for a needle in a haystack. A squadron of frigates fitted with the latest submarine detection devices began combing this expanse square by square, assisted by two survey ships. Whenever a hopeful contact was made, the rescue ship *Reclaim* was moored over the spot and her divers went down to investigate.

It was a slow and frustrating task for Shelford and his company, but they stuck at it in all weathers. Time and again, as he has related in his authoritative book *Subsunk*, the diver, 'a lone and grotesque figure, groped his way over a rusted and barnacled wreck and told us the depressing news that once again we had not found *Affray*.' There was only a few hours in each twenty-four, the periods of slack water, when the *Reclaim* could be moored and her divers work; and their time on the bottom, two hundred feet down, was measured in minutes.

When the search had been in progress for about five weeks someone at the Admiralty Research Laboratory had the bright idea of using an underwater television camera which was then available and could be taken down to depths of two hundred feet and more. This speeded things up considerably; if the television screen showed an old wreck or the hull of a surface ship there was no need to proceed further, and the *Reclaim* moved on to investigate another contact.

By mid-June the search had moved to an area some thirty miles north of Guernsey, and one day a diver's metallic voice came up the telephone to say that he could see a gleaming white rail. This was the first time anything had been found not covered in rust. The diver was at once hauled up and the television camera sent down. The men watching the screen saw a picture of the rails round a submarine's gun-turret and then, amid mounting excitement, letters appeared one by one: first a Y and then A–R–F–F–A. A triumphant signal was made to C-in-C Portsmouth announcing that the *Affray* had been found.

So far so good. But the question as to why she was lying on the bottom with seventy-five corpses inside her, 278 feet down and somewhat south of her expected track, still remained to be answered. Divers went down to the wreck and could find no evidence of damage or anything pointing to a cause of the disaster. All the hatches were closed; the periscope usually used when cruising at periscope depth and the detection radar aerial were both raised. No attempt seemed to have been made to open the escape hatches nor to release the indicator buoys. Whatever had happened to the crew had come very quickly.

The underwater camera was lowered to probe about the wreck and it showed that both pairs of hydroplanes were at 'Hard-arise', which meant efforts had been made to hold the submarine up; while both pointers of the bridge telegraph were at 'Stop', indicating that the captain had expected to hit the sea-bottom hard. The *Affray* was lying with only a slight list to port.

However, further examination found that the snort-tube was snapped off a few feet above deck level and was leaning over the hull. The break was so clean that it was obvious the material had failed. Nevertheless, the length of snort-tube had to be recovered for expert examination. Perhaps it would show signs of having been hit by a ship or by floating wreckage.

A salvage ship went across the Channel to assist the *Reclaim* if necessary. There was a heavy sea running during the day but it fell away towards evening, when the *Reclaim* was safely moored and was flying a signal warning shipping to keep clear. Just as preliminary operations were beginning, the great liner *Queen Elizabeth* was seen working up speed on her way down-Channel, sending a huge wash towards the *Reclaim*. 'Please go slow' was signalled to her, and at once she eased right down and dipped her ensign to the salvage ships as she slipped past to the north of them.

It took two days to grapple and hoist the snort-tube to the surface. Shelford and the engineer officer of the *Reclaim* made a thorough examination when it lay on deck, but could find no sign of it having been hit. It had just snapped clean off – and this was confirmed by expert laboratory tests after it was landed at Portsmouth. That being so, the intake valve fitted at the point where the snort entered the pressure hull should have shut itself. This valve which brought air to the engines was designed to shut as soon as the snort was beneath the water – a most necessary safety precaution. Moreover, if for some unknown reason the valve had remained open when the snort snapped, the *Affray* would most likely have sunk by the stern. Yet she had been found undamaged aft and lying on the bottom on a fairly even keel.

Nevertheless the position of this important valve, whether it was shut or open, had to be determined. The *Reclaim* returned to the scene of the wreck and divers went down again. They found it was impossible to get near the valve without taking some drastic action, such as blasting. And the *Affray*'s list to port had greatly increased, making operations very hazardous for the divers; she might roll over and crush one of them. So operations were called off – more, the decision was taken at a high level not to try and salvage the *Affray*. The reason for this decision has never been disclosed. In November 1951 the Admiralty announced that there was insufficient evidence to determine the cause of the loss of the *Affray*. Such is the authorized version. To the public, the cause of her sinking and the reason why none of her crew even attempted to escape is still a mystery.

The disaster had at least proved that the Subsunk organization functioned most efficiently, and that every possible aid can now be brought to the crew of a sunken submarine in the shortest time possible.

Bibliography

Bennett, Geoffrey, *Naval Battles of the First World War* (Batsford, 1968)

Carr, W.G., *By Guess and By God* (Hutchinson, 1930)

Durand de la Penne, Luigi, 'The Italian Attack on the Alexandria Naval Base' (*U.S. Naval Institute Proceedings*, February 1956)

Edwards, Kenneth, *We Dive at Dawn* (Rich and Cowan, 1939)

Frank, Wolfgang, *The Sea Wolves* (Weidenfeld and Nicolson, 1955)

Hart, Sydney, *Submarine Upholder* (Oldbourne, 1960)

Hezlet, Sir Arthur, *The Submarine and Sea Power* (Peter Davies, 1967)

Jameson, William, *The Most Formidable Thing* (Hart-Davis, 1965)

Kemp, Peter, *H.M. Submarines* (Jenkins, 1952)

Laurens, Adolphe, *Histoire de la Guerre Sous-Marine Allemande (1914–18)* (Paris, 1930)

Macintyre, Donald, *U-Boat Killer* (Weidenfeld and Nicolson, 1956)

Macintyre, Donald, *The Battle of the Atlantic* (Batsford, 1961)

Mordal, Jacques, *25 Siècles de Guerre sur Mer* (Paris, 1959)

Noli, Jean, *Les Loups de l'Amiral* (Paris, 1970)

Porten, E.P. von der, *The German Navy in World War Two* (Arthur Barker, 1970)

Sellwood, A.V., *Dynamite for Hire* (Werner Laurie, 1956)

Shankland, P. and Hunter, A., *Dardanelles Patrol* (Collins, 1964)

Shelford, W.O., *Subsunk* (Harrap, 1960)

Stafford, Edward P., *The Far and the Deep* (Arthur Barker, 1968)

Waldron, T. and Gleeson, J., *The Frogmen* (Evans, 1950)

Warren, C. and Benson, J., *'The Admiralty Regrets. . .'* (Harrap, 1958)

Warren, C. and Benson, J., *Above Us the Waves* (Harrap, 1953)

Werner, H.A., *Iron Coffins* (Arthur Barker, 1970)

Winton, John, (Ed.), *Freedom's Battle: Vol. 1, The War at Sea, 1939-45* (Hutchinson, 1970)

Young, Edward, *One of our Submarines* (Hart-Davis, 1952)